THE TROY STETINA® SERIES

METAL RHYTHM GUITAR

VOLUME TWO

Cover guitar courtesy of Cascio Music

ISBN 0-7935-0959-9

7777 W. BLUEMOUND RD. P.O. BOX 13819 MILWAUKEE, WI 53213

www.troystetina.com

Visit Hal Leonard Online at **www.halleonard.com**

ABOUT THE AUTHOR

Photo Credit: Brian Beckwith

Troy Stetina is an internationally recognized guitarist, solo artist, and music educator. Specializing in rock, metal, shred, and classical-electric guitar, he has authored more than 40 book/audio and DVD methods that have guided a generation of players toward excellence and guitar mastery. Troy endorses PRS guitars, the Dimis Troy Stetina Custom Signature guitar, Engl amps, Lampifier microphones, and Dunlop strings.

Visit Troy online at www.troystetina.com for lessons, tips, videos, tour and masterclass event dates as well as current product information and full bibliography/discography.

Music CDs:
Second Soul *Beyond the Infinite*
Dimension X *Implications of a Genetic Defense*
Troy Stetina *Exottica*

CREDITS AND ACKNOWLEDGMENTS

Guitars and bass: Troy Stetina
Drums: Brian Reidinger (all songs in Volumes 1 and 2, except "Babylon")
All songs and examples written and arranged by Troy Stetina
Mixed at Gemini Studios, Faribault, MN (except "Babylon")
Produced by Troy Stetina and Brian Reidinger
Digital editing at "In the Groove," Minneapolis, MN

Equipment:
    Guitars: Jackson soloist (with Sustainiac GA-2, Duncan Custom pickup); Washburn MG-700
    Amps: Marshall 100 watt, Mk II; Marshall 50 watt, JCM 800 series; Marshall 4x12 cabinets
    Pedals: Boss PD-1 (Distortion pedal), Ibanez TS10 Tube Screamer
    Alesis HR-16 Drum machine (on all examples)

Many people were involved in the production of, or had some input into, this guitar method, and they all deserve thanks. Thanks to all the people at Hal Leonard Corporation. And a special thank you goes to the love of my life, Shauna. Also, thanks to Brian Reidinger, Don Dokken, Washburn Guitars, Wolf Marshall and Guitar One magazine, and all the creative musicians that forge ahead, making the music that breaks new ground, keeps us interested, entertained, and sometimes even makes us think about where we are and what we are doing. And finally, thanks to all of you—the emerging guitarists of tomorrow. Ultimately it is you who have made it possible for me to do what I do. Thank you!

WELCOME TO THE "TROY STETINA SERIES"

The *Troy Stetina Series* is a complete system for mastering metal and building solid musicianship. The books, methods and videos of the series cover the full spectrum of playing from the beginning all the way up to the most advanced rhythm and lead concepts, fretboard pyrotechnics, theory, melodic principles, songwriting, and how to develop your own personal lead style. In short, this series is designed to take you to a professional level of playing.

Brief descriptions of the books and videos of this series appear at the end of this book. You can use this to help you navigate through the series and select what is best for you. Keep in mind that it is generally best to use several complementary books at a time, in order to have plenty of variety in your practice. Each book comes with accompanying audio so it may be used individually as well as with the guidance of a teacher.

 This symbol indicates the audio track number for the examples in that section.

FOREWORD

Metal Rhythm Guitar Volume 2 continues the Metal Rhythm Guitar method with the same playing-intensive format. You'll learn more advanced chording, riffs and rhythms used by classic and cutting edge bands including **Stone Temple Pilots, Guns 'N' Roses, Live, Nirvana, The Offspring, Metallica, Ministry, Pantera, White Zombie, Alice in Chains, Soundgarden, Pearl Jam, Bush, Candlebox, Collective Soul, Ozzy Osbourne, Van Halen** and more. And, at the same time, you'll be completing that solid musical foundation and technique that you need to master metal rhythm guitar playing.

Specifically, this volume covers full barre chords, seventh, ninth, suspended and add chords, inverted and slash chords, diads, chord progression theory and harmonized scales, alternating and strum picking, accent picking, sixteenth note figures, offbeat accents, triplets, rhythmic patterns, shuffle rhythms, other time signatures, dropped D tuning, and more.

Once again, all of the concepts are applied in real playing situations over a range of metal styles in six more songs—"Lucky Day," "In the Spirit," "Nervosa," "Monsterfunker," "Demon's Waltz," as well as the instrumental tune "Babylon," which concludes Volume 2.

So crank up your amp and let's tear into it!

 Tuning notes.

CHAPTER 7

"E" FORM BARRE CHORDS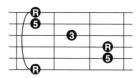

We can create moveable major and minor chord shapes from the corresponding open chord shapes, in the same way that we made our first moveable power chords back in chapter one. These full, moveable chord shapes are called *barre chords* because one finger lays, or bars, across the strings. Because our first barre chords below are based on the open E major and minor chords, we can call them *E-form* barre chords.

Play E major using your *second, third,* and *fourth* fingers, thereby leaving your first finger free, as shown below on the left. Then, shift everything up a fret. Lay your first finger across the string at the first fret (raising the open strings one fret as well), and you have an F major chord. Shift everything up to the third fret and you have G major, at the fifth fret its A major, and so on. The chord tones—root, third, fifth—are labelled within the voicing to the right.

First, play E major like this:

Then, shift up the neck and bar:

Moveable Major Shape

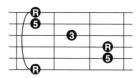

TIP: Notice the power chord within this major shape (on the lower three strings). Now focus on the location of the third. It is this major third that makes the chord major. Finally, look at the top strings and notice that they are simply octaves of the fifth and root.

Now let's look at the moveable minor shape, based on E minor.

First, play E minor like this:

Then, shift up the neck and bar:

Moveable Minor Shape

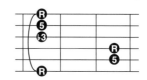

TIP: Notice that the minor third tone, or ♭3, appears one fret below the position of the major third.

1

	E	Em	F	Fm	G	Gm	A	Am	B	Bm	C	Cm	D	Dm
clean	⊓	⊓	⊓	⊓	⊓	⊓	⊓	⊓	⊓	⊓	⊓	⊓	⊓	⊓

```
      E  Em    F  Fm    G  Gm    A  Am    B  Bm    C  Cm    D   Dm
   clean
 T   0  0    1  1    3  3    5  5    7  7    8  8    10  10
 A   0  0    1  1    3  3    5  5    7  7    8  8    10  10
     1  0    2  1    4  3    6  5    8  7    9  8    11  10
 B   2  2    3  3    5  5    7  7    9  9    10 10   12  12
     2  2    3  3    5  5    7  7    9  9    10 10   12  12
     0  0    1  1    3  3    5  5    7  7    8  8    10  10
```

"A" FORM BARRE CHORDS ◆**3**

We can similarly "bar up" the open A major and minor chords to create moveable A-form shapes. Again, notice the voicing of the chord tones.

Play A major like this:

Then, shift up the neck and bar:

Moveable Major Shape

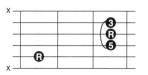

Play A minor like this:

Then, shift up the neck and bar:

Moveable Minor Shape

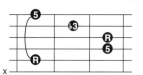

2

```
      A  Am    B  Bm    C  Cm    D  Dm    E  Em    F  Fm    G   Gm
   clean
        0       2       3       5       7       8       10
 T   2  1    4  3    5  4    7  6    9  8    10 9    12  11
 A   2  2    4  4    5  5    7  7    9  9    10 10   12  12
     2  2    4  4    5  5    7  7    9  9    10 10   12  12
 B   0  0    2  2    3  3    5  5    7  7    8  8    10  10
```

5

THE STRUMMING APPROACH ◆ 4

Throughout Volume 1, eighth notes have been played almost entirely with downstrokes of the pick. Another picking technique is the use of an alternating, down/up/down pattern. When applied to chords, this is known as a *strumming* pattern. You can hear this approach at work in such songs as "Patience" by Guns 'N' Roses, "About a Girl" by Nirvana, or "Interstate Love Song" by Stone Temple Pilots, for example.

The first example below demonstrates the basic strumming approach. Pick every downbeat with a downstroke and every upbeat with an upstroke, so your foot and hand move together. Also, clean up the sound a bit for these examples by rolling the volume knob down on your guitar.

> TIP: Imagine a string is tied between your pick and your foot. For this example, pretend that you must keep this imaginary string taught by moving your foot and hand up and down exactly together.

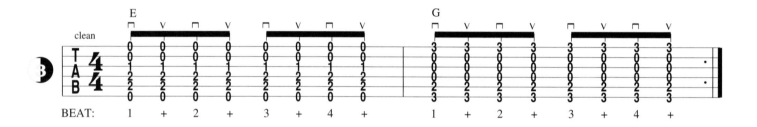

Now let's throw a syncopation into it. Don't pick the strings on the tied downbeat, but make the corresponding downstroke motion nonetheless, to maintain the alternating pattern. In other words, miss the strings for the second note of the tied pair.

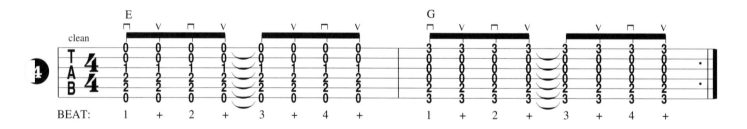

Rests are played just like ties, with regard to the alternating picking pattern. The only difference, of course, is that you want to stop the strings on the rests.

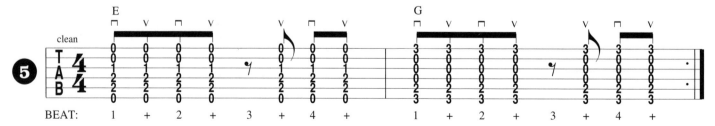

The following examples use some common strumming patterns. Example 6 uses open chords in a simple two-chord progression à la Nirvana. First its played clean, then distortion is kicked in on the repeat. Example 7 uses full barre chords, and example 8 incorporates power chords and rests.

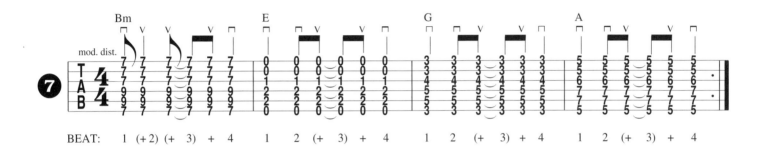

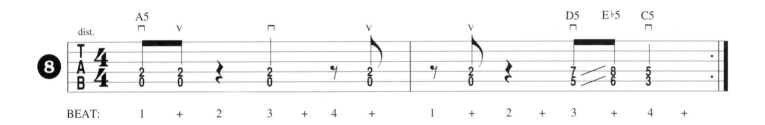

Left hand mutes are often used in place of rests in these strumming-type rhythms. Example 9 adds some left hand mutes into the riff shown above as example 8, giving us something similar to the driving riff at the heart of Collective Souls's alternative-pop-grunge tune, "Gel."

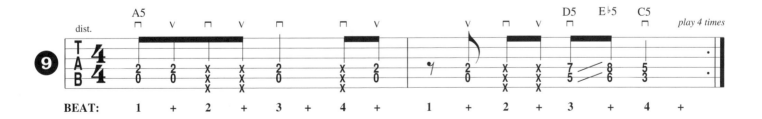

NATURAL HARMONIC "MUTES" ◆**5**

When left hand mutes are played with just one finger touching a particular string, higher pitched harmonics of that string are created, rather than the percussive "click." These harmonics, known as natural harmonics, are often used in place of pure click-mutes for their effect. This technique can be heard in riffs from Ozzy Osbourne to Stone Temple Pilots, and is especially present in the punk-pop-metal of bands like The Offspring, Nirvana and Weezer.

Form an F power chord at the first fret, but don't press the strings down to the fretboard. Instead hold the strings mute and strike the lower strings. You'll hear a high pitched noise, or squeal. As you slowly slide up the neck, notice that different pitches are created at different points.

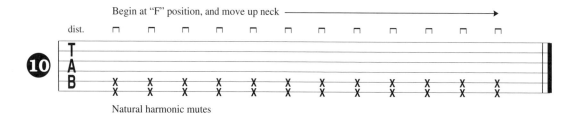

You are hearing harmonics of the open strings. For our purposes here, it doesn't really matter exactly what pitches are being created because we are using these harmonics as a type of effect, without regard to their specific pitches. Just think of them as simply "sloppy" left-hand mutes. (See *Metal Lead Guitar Volume 1*, Chapter Six, to learn about using natural harmonics as specific notes.)

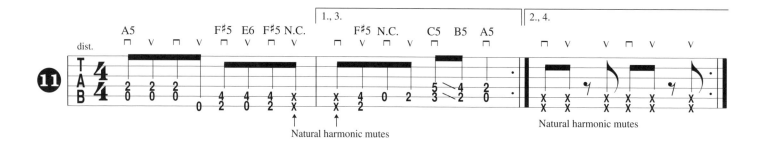

TIP: The key difference as to whether you produce "percussive mutes" or "harmonic mutes" depends on how many fingers you use to mute the strings. Touch the string in just one place (with just one finger) and you'll likely get a natural harmonic. Touch it in two or more places (with three fingers, for example) and you'll get a percussive click. Try both techniques and notice the different sounds you can create.

RIFFS VS. PROGRESSIONS 6

What's the difference between a riff and a progression? These terms can seem a bit fuzzy and imprecise at times, but they do have fundamentally distinct meanings. Understanding these distinctions will help you make more sense of the songs you learn.

Riffs

A riff is a short, repeated phrase that is structurally significant in a song. Because they are short, riffs create a static tonal center. For example, if it's in the key of E, the pitch of E is implied throughout, whether the riff consists of single notes or chords. This excerpt from "As Darkness Gathers" is a good example of a phrase that is a riff—in this case, its a chordal riff in E.

Progressions

A progression, on the other hand, is a sequence of chords that goes by slower. Slow enough in fact, that you will hear an overall tonal movement. The pro-gression forms an underlying framework for a melody which weaves above it. The phrase on the right, from "The Tao of Metal," is a good example of a phrase that falls into the category of a progression—in this case, it's an E-G-D-A progression.

Moving riffs through progressions

So riffs are smaller, progressions are bigger. One way to illustrate this is by the fact that you can move a riff *through* a progression. Look back at example 71 in Volume 1 for a moment. There, an evil two-bar riff moves through blues changes in E—that is, an E-A-E-B-E chord progression.

For all of you who didn't bother to dig up Volume 1, I'll give you another chance. Get it out now and look at that example! (It's on page 41.) Good. Now notice that although an A chord does appear within each riff in E, it doesn't have the same weight—or create the sense of movement—as the A portion of the progression. Play it and you'll hear what I mean. In the riff, A is just a *passing chord*. Rely on your ear to tell you when the progression really moves.

As this illustrates, the progression may not be the same as the chord sequence. You usually have to dig a little to see the bare essence of the progression. Basically, knock out all passing notes and/or chords to get to the heart of the progression itself. So remember, the term *progression* is a larger concept and refers to tonal movement, not just a sequence of chords in a riff.

Where the twain meet

Imagine speeding up a progression—or adding more and more passing notes—until you reach a point where you have *nothing but* passing notes and/or chords. You wind up with a static tonal center and there is no real *progression,* or movement. Presto. Your progression has become a riff! So these categories are not black and white, but there is a range of greys in between; where they intersect. Most often, however, riffs and progressions are quite distinct from one another and therefore they remain very useful concepts.

RIFF FORM

As you've just read, one of the important aspects of a riff is *repetition*. Remember, a riff is a short, *repeated* figure which is a structurally significant part of a song. So let's take a closer look at the different ways riffs may be found to repeat. In other words, we're going to consider the *form,* or structure, of riffs themselves.

Just as overall sections of music can be labelled with the letters A, B, C, etc., to describe a song's form, the same letters may be used to describe the parts of a riff as well. Remember, these letters are variables—like "x" and "y" in algebra—so they can stand for anything. Simple repetition of a riff (four times, for example) could be represented AAAA. Alternating with a different ending makes the form ABAB. Multiple endings create an ABAC structure. The form AAAB is also common. Listen for these forms in the four variations of the riff below.

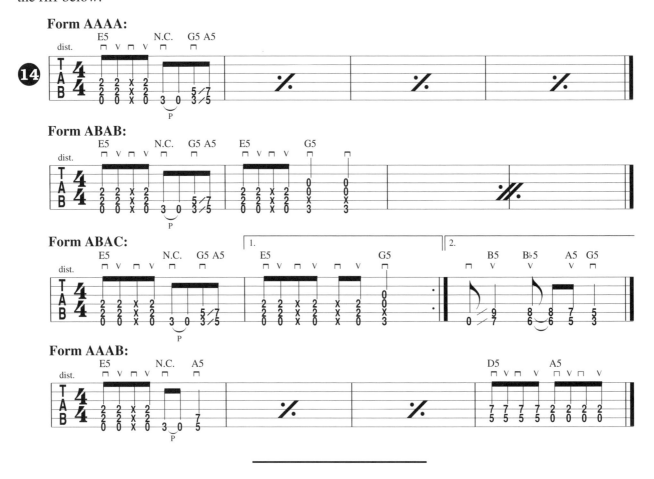

"Lucky Day"—the first song of Volume 2—is an upbeat, alternative-pop-grunge-metal groove. As in Volume One, the song appears first in full arrangement, then it is repeated without any rhythm guitars so you can practice with it, record yourself with it, etc. The verse and chorus melodies are played by a lead guitar to more clearly define the song's structure (so you don't get lost) and to give it a full, realistic song feel.

"Lucky Day" uses a chordal, strumming approach. It contains riff and chord progression sections as distinct as night and day. The riff is a one-bar chordal variety in E, sandwiching verse lines in B♭. The chorus is a fast-moving Em-C-G-D progression.

In the largest sense, the structure of the entire song is verse/chorus/verse/chorus/bridge-solo/chorus, or ABABCB. Listen for this typical overall song structure first. This is what the letters in the transcription correspond to. But look a little closer and you'll see that the verse sections we just labelled as "A" are actually made up of a *riff/verse line/riff/verse line/riff* structure. We could see this as an ABABA form. (Don't confuse these letters with those of the previous level. Here, "A" represents the riff and "B" represents the verse lines.) And finally, dialing in the microscope to yet a higher level of magnification, the riff itself could be described by AAAB. Can you figure out what form best describes the chorus?

LUCKY DAY 8 9
(Song #7)

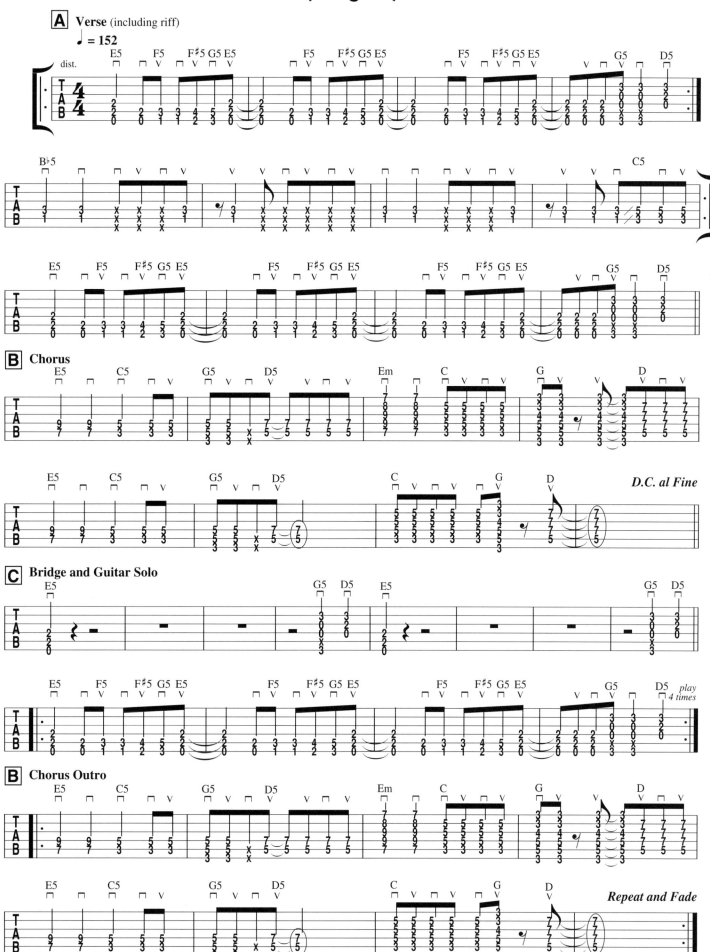

CHAPTER 8

BACKGROUND THEORY

In a piece of music, there is generally one pitch, or note, that acts as the *tonal center*. It is called the tonic note, or the keynote. It can be any pitch, but the most common in rock and metal is undoubtedly E and A, followed by D, G and F♯. (The tonal center in "Lucky Day," for example, was E.) Whatever pitch it is, the tonal center is home base and the rest of the notes and chords can be viewed as revolving around that central pitch. A chord built upon the tonal center has a special significance and we call it the *tonic chord*.

The other notes and chords which revolve around this tonal center can do so in basically two different ways. They can be drawn mostly from the major scale, in which case we say the song is in a *major key*. Or they can be drawn mostly from the minor scale, in which case we say it is in a *minor key*. Of course these are not the only two kinds of scales on which a song may be based, but nearly all other scales can be classified as either "major types" or "minor types." Think of major and minor as being the two main categories.

As you already know, major and minor are generally regarded as opposites—major is bright and happy, minor is dark and sad. We'll look at major keys in this chapter. Then, in the following chapter, we'll dig into minor keys.

BUILDING CHORDS IN A MAJOR KEY 🔟

Let's start with E major. Below, an E major scale pattern is shown stretched out on a single string. The steps of the scale are numbered 1, 2, 3, 4, 5, 6, 7 to reflect each note's relative position to the tonal center, E.

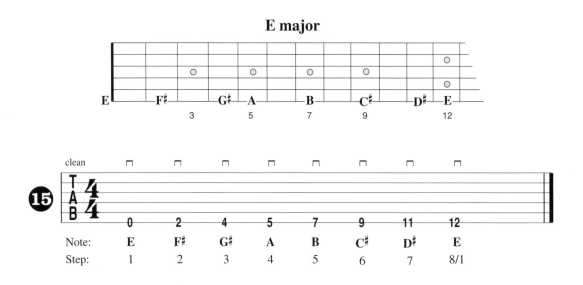

These notes—E, F♯, G♯, A, B, C♯, D♯, E—*are natural to*, or found within, the key of E major. All other notes are outside the key.

Now let's build a chord on each note, or step, of this scale. We will have an E chord, F♯ chord, G♯ chord, A chord, B chord, C♯ chord, and D♯ chord. But what type of chord will each be? To find out, we need to *harmonize* the scale. This is a process of stacking up intervals of thirds to build chords from the ground up, using just the notes within this scale and no "outsiders."

An *interval of a third* is two steps of the scale. So the distance between steps 1 and 3 is a third, as well as from 2 to 4, 3 to 5, etc. But not all thirds are created equal. Some are four frets, or major thirds, and others are only three frets, or *minor thirds*. For example, E to G♯ is four frets, so it is a major third. F♯ to A is only three frets, so it is a minor third. Label the types of thirds in the spaces below, as either major or minor thirds.

Thirds in the key of E major

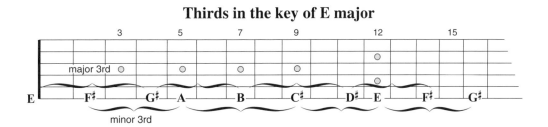

The third beginning on step 1 (or, E) is a _____ third.

The third beginning on step 2 (or, F♯) is a _____ third.

The third beginning on step 3 (or, G♯) is a _____ third.

The third beginning on step 4 (or, A) is a _____ third.

The third beginning on step 5 (or, B) is a _____ third.

The third beginning on step 6 (or, C♯) is a _____ third.

The third beginning on step 7 (or, D♯) is a _____ third.

The third beginning on step 8 (or, E) is a _____ third.

Now we can stack them up. We'll move our E scale up an octave, to the fourth string, and put the thirds on the next higher string so we can see all of these intervals as diads (or, two-note chords). Notice the specific shape of both the major and minor thirds, below, in diad form. If you filled in the blanks above correctly, you'll notice that the sequence here is the same.

Harmonized thirds in key of E major, as diads

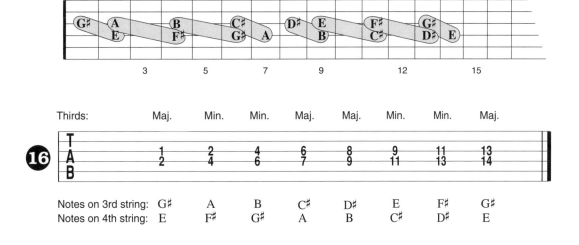

Next, we can stack another third on top of the diads to create *triads* (or, three-note chords). The bottom note of each triad, found on the D string, is the root of that triad or chord. The middle note, found on the G string, is the *third* of that triad or chord. The top note, on the B string, is the *fifth* of that triad or chord.

Harmonized triads in E major

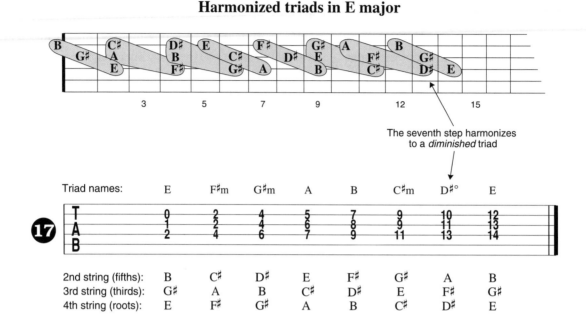

The seventh step harmonizes to a *diminished* triad

2nd string (fifths):	B	C♯	D♯	E	F♯	G♯	A	B
3rd string (thirds):	G♯	A	B	C♯	D♯	E	F♯	G♯
4th string (roots):	E	F♯	G♯	A	B	C♯	D♯	E

Below, the chords in E major are shown in their full barre chord voicings. If you look closely, you can see each of the triad shapes which you've just played, hiding within these barre chords.

Roman numerals indicate each chord's position within the key, relative to the tonic. Capital numerals indicate major chords, small numerals indicate minor chords, and the diminished chord has an additional "o" to indicate that it has a diminished, or flatted, fifth.

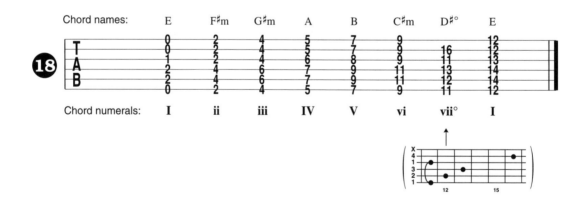

If this harmonizing business seems confusing, don't worry. Your ear will tell you that the chords are right—you will hear the major scale move as you play through them. The important thing is that you learn this pattern of chords.

> TIP: Memorize the fact that in a major key, the chords I, IV, and V are major, while ii, iii, and vi are minor and the vii° is diminished.

The following progressions are in the key of E major. See if some of these familiar-sounding progressions bring to mind any songs you've heard. Although you could play all the chords rooted on the sixth string, the following progressions use chords rooted on the fifth string as well. Note the corresponding scale relationships—shown to the right—and memorize the pattern they make. After you play each example, write in the correct chord numerals.

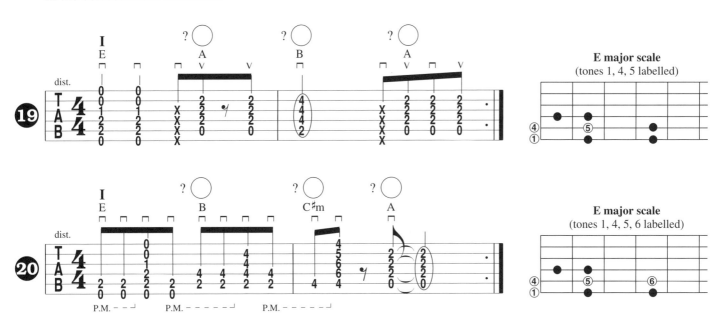

When the third of a chord is omitted, we'll add a small "5" to the roman numeral, indicating that it is a power chord. But we'll still use either the capital or small roman numeral as appropriate. Even though the thirds aren't actually played, they are implied. Because the progression itself follows a major key pattern, the thirds would also follow the same key *if they were played*. And often, in fact, the thirds *are* found in the vocal melody.

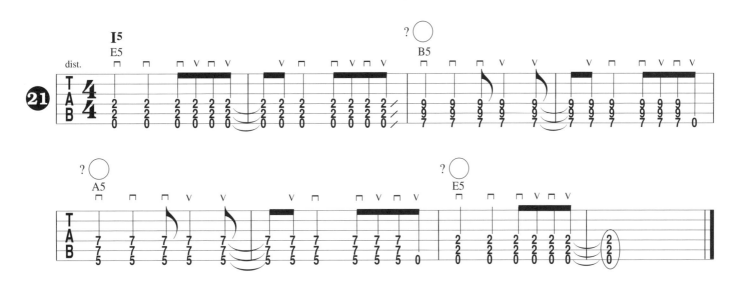

Progressions: Ex. 19, I-IV-V-IV; Ex. 20, I-V-vi-IV; Ex. 21, I⁵-V⁵-vi⁵-IV⁵

The advantage of seeing progressions in terms of their chord numerals becomes apparent when we begin changing keys, or *transposing*. First, let's transpose our set of chords into another key, by simply sliding the pattern of chords to place the "I" on the new tonic position. Below, our harmonized chord pattern is shown transposed into the keys of G and A.

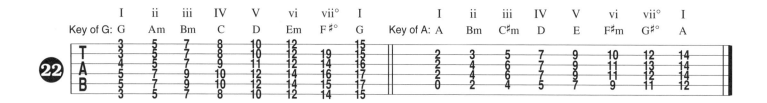

You can see from the chords above that a I-V-vi-IV progression, for example, corresponds to the chords G-D-Em-C in the key of G and A-E-F♯m-D in the key of A. Below, this progression has been transposed into first G and then A. Notice how the relative pattern remains the same, and it sounds basically the same except a little higher.

TIP: Changing keys within a piece of music is known as *modulation*. Example 23 modulates from G to A, while maintaining the same I-V-vi-IV progression.

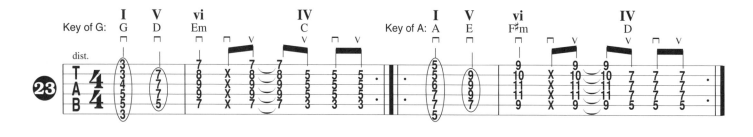

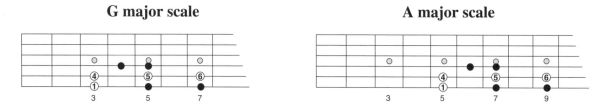

TIP: Actually, you don't need to find and label every chord in a key to transpose a progression. You can simply slide the whole pattern of chords to the new position, maintaining the same relative spacing. The scale patterns above, show this graphically. This is the easiest and most direct way to transpose any progression.

Chords may be raised or lowered an octave without affecting the progression in terms of its roman numeral identification. For example, this same I-V-vi-IV progression in A which you've just played, is shown below in new pair of pants—all in power chords and with the vi chord lowered an octave.

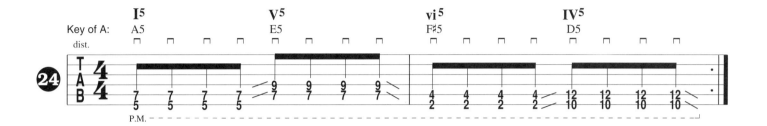

When the I chord is shifted up to an octave, both the IV and V chords will be left *below* the I chord. Here, this relative position of I, IV, and V is shown in the key of E.

E major

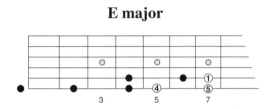

Now let's shift this pattern down two frets, and we have I, IV, and V in the key of *D*. Example 25, below uses this in a progression, similar to that used in the choruses of both Bush's "All Comes Down" and Soul Asylum's "Misery."

D major

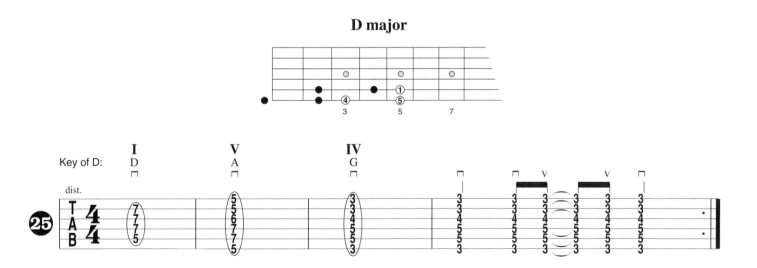

THE ♭VII VARIATION ◆13

As you already know, the chord built on the seventh step of the major scale turns out to be diminished. This is rarely used, however. Rather a ♭VII chord is generally substituted. Since a major scale with a flatted seventh step is known as a "Mixolydian mode," we can call this a *Mixolydian variation*—or a ♭VII variation.

In the key of E, the ♭VII chord is D major. (If you want to see this for yourself, look back at the triads on page 14, flat the root of the D♯ diminished chord one fret and you're left with a D major triad.) The chords of E major are shown below with the ♭VII variation.

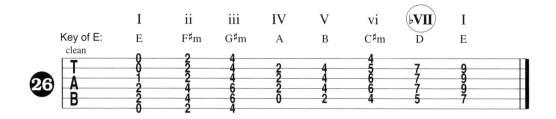

The chord relationships I, IV, and ♭VII are even more common in rock and metal than are I, IV, V. In various sequences and in different keys, I-IV-♭VII can be found at the heart of Guns 'N' Roses' "Sweet Child" and "Paradise City," Van Halen's "Panama" and "Black and Blue," AC/DC's classic "Back in Black," Live's "Lightning Crashes," and Collective Soul's "Shine," to cite just a few prominent instances.

See if you can recognize any progressions from the songs mentioned above, within the following examples. Again, write in the correct roman numerals for each progression.

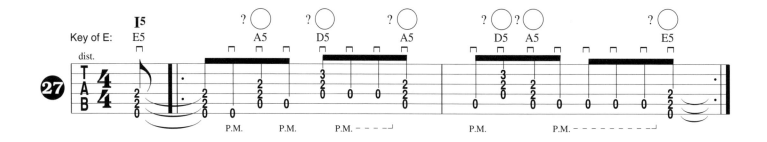

E Mixolydian

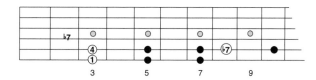

G Mixolydian

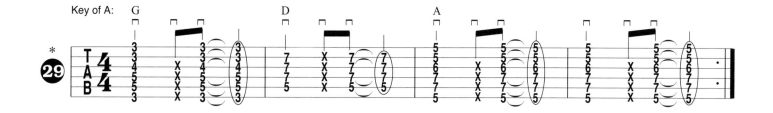

A Mixolydian

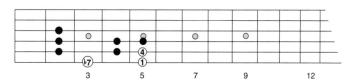

*Omitted from recording.

The fretboard can seem a little complicated at first, because each chord can be played in different places. So the same progression may appear differently. And at the same time, a certain pattern can form different progressions, depending on which note is considered the tonic. (For example A, D, and E are I, IV, and V in the key of A, but they become IV, ♭VII, and I in the key of E.) But that's part of the beauty of the guitar. There are so many options. Just learn each progression you come across on a case by case basis, and over time, everything will fall into place.

TIP: When you are learning a song, first identify the tonic (or key). Then determine the chord numerals of the remaining chords, and memorize their pattern. Each particular relationship has its own sound, so eventually, when you become familiar with them, you'll be able to recognize each one purely by ear. And because you also will know how they appear on the fretboard, you'll be able to play any song simply by listening—before you even touch your guitar! This is known as developing *relative pitch*.

"SUS" AND "ADD" CHORDS ◆14◆

Suspended 4th and *suspended 2nd* chords, commonly abbreviated and referred to as "sus4" and "sus2," are chords in which the third of the chord has been replaced with either a fourth or second tone, respectively. This gives these chord a characteristic suspended feeling. The chord formula for a sus4 chord is 1, 4, 5, and for a sus2 chord is 1, 2, 5.

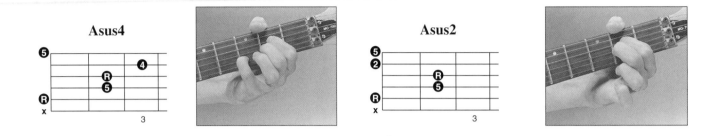

Hold the sus4 chord in example 30 and notice its characteristic sound. It is as if the fourth wants to fall down to the third. But the chord resists, or suspends this natural inclination, hence the name *suspended* fourth. Then play the sus2. This time you can hear the suspension of the second wanting to pull up to the third.

Below are moveable barre chord shapes for sus4 and sus2, with the root on the fifth string.

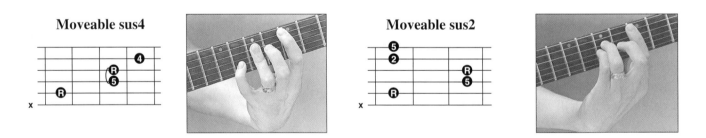

The sus chords in the following progression simply add some variety and texture to the chords.

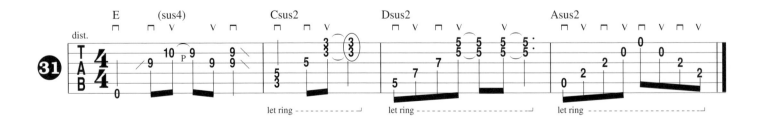

An *add* chord is simply a chord to which a non-chord tone has been added. So E add⁹ is an E major chord with a 9th thrown in, and Em add⁹ is be an Em chord with an added 9th. Sometimes add⁹ is called add² because the 9th and 2nd are actually the same note. But add⁹ is usually a better name because it suggests that the added note is in a higher octave—which is almost always the case—and not right next to the root.

Some common add⁹s are shown below. Notice that the 9th/2nd tone always appears two frets above the position of an octave root.

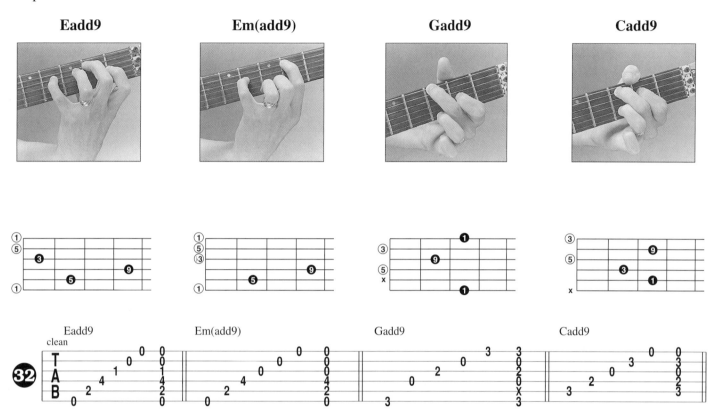

Eadd9 **Em(add9)** **Gadd9** **Cadd9**

COMMON TONES AND MELODIC FRAGMENTS ◆15

The following progressions use sus and add chords. Example 33 features a haunting, arpeggiated progression with an open string *common tone*. That is, the B is common to—or found within—each chord. Example 34 uses sus and add chords to create a moving melody line within the progression. Notice how the same, short piece of melody, or *melodic fragment*, found in the first measure (over A) is re-introduced over a G chord in the third measure. Then in the last measure, the same melodic fragment appears again, but this time it's transposed to make the same relationship to D as the original fragment was to A.

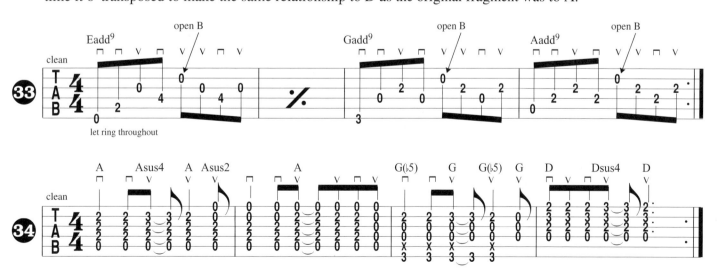

21

SLASH AND INVERTED CHORDS ◆16

No, *slash chords* are not those preferred by Slash, lead guitarist of Guns 'N' Roses. (Although that's a good guess.) They are chords in which a note other than the root is the lowest note in the chord.

The following riff is similar to Stone Temple Pilot's "Wicked Garden." Notice that the G5 chords sandwiched between A5's maintain the A note in the bass. We label this using a slash symbol—G5/A— which is read "G5 over A." In this case, slash chords have resulted from holding a common tone in the bass (known as a *pedal tone*) throughout the riff.

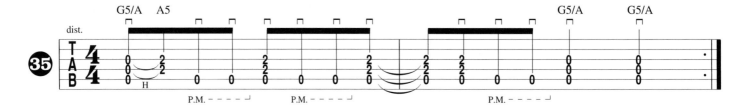

When the note in the bass of the chord happens to be a chord tone (other than the root), we have a special type of slash chord called an *inversion.*

First inversion means that the root has been raised up an octave—turning the chord "upside down," or inverting it—and thereby leaving the third as the lowest note. Look at the open G chord on the right. Without the root on the bottom, the lowest note is B. So this is a first inversion G major chord, written G/B.

G, first inversion

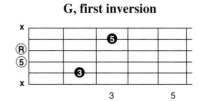

Here is another way to play that first inversion G major chord, using a moveable, two-note chord shape. This major inversion shape is actually a minor 6th diad. Notice the position of the fifth and low root, even though you won't actually be playing them.

G, first inversion, moveable

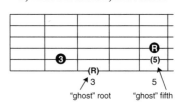

Example 36 uses moveable, first inversion major diads. Notice how the bass note moves *chromatically,* through consecutive half steps.

> TIP: Always look to the position of the lower "ghost" root to name these first inversion chords.

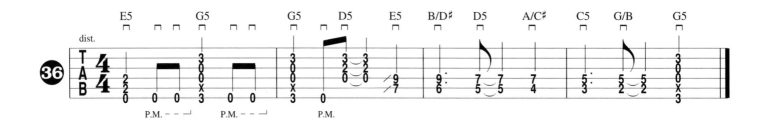

If we invert a first inversion chord again, and raise the third up an octave as well, we are left with the *fifth* in the bass. This is called *second inversion*. The slash chords in example 37 are in second inversion.

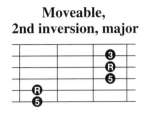

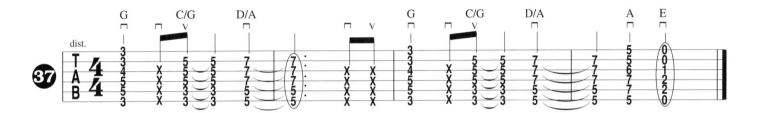

If we were to invert a second inversion chord again, our chord would be back to having the root in the bass, just an octave higher (assuming it to be a three-note chord). This "normal" version of a chord—with the root in the bass—is called *root position*.

HALF TIME (INTRO TO SIXTEENTH NOTES) ⬦

Half time means that the drums play a half-speed groove, while the guitar part remains unchanged. This gives the feeling that the underlying beat is suddenly going at half the written speed. Listen to example 38 and notice the apparent tempo change at the half time indication.

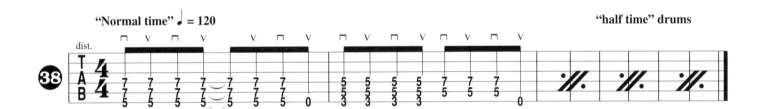

This could be written by actually changing the tempo to one-half and doubling the speed of the notes. Whole notes become half notes, half become quarter, quarter become eighth, and eighth become sixteenth notes.

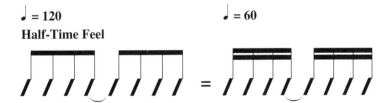

Sixteenth notes aren't difficult. They're simply eighth notes in half time. In the following song, we'll use eighth-note rhythms in half time as an easy (and sneaky) way of getting you introduced to the feel of sixteenth note grooves, while still reading just eighth notes.

"In the Spirit" has a half-time ballad feel somewhere between the style of Live and Guns 'N' Roses. It is in the key of D, primarily using I, ♭VII, IV major-type progressions, with an occasional appearance of the V chord. Write in the correct chord numerals over each significant chord change. (D, Dsus2 and Dsus4, for example, can all be considered as I.)

It is arranged for two guitars—guitar 1 uses a moderately distorted tone and favors open chords, while guitar 2 uses heavier distortion with power chords and barre chords. Learn each part and notice how they interact. The form is intro/verse/pre-chorus/verse/pre-chorus/chorus/solo/chorus, or A-AB-ABC-D-C. Remember, each measure here gets only *two* slower, compound beats.

IN THE SPIRIT ◆18◆ ◆19◆
(Song #8)

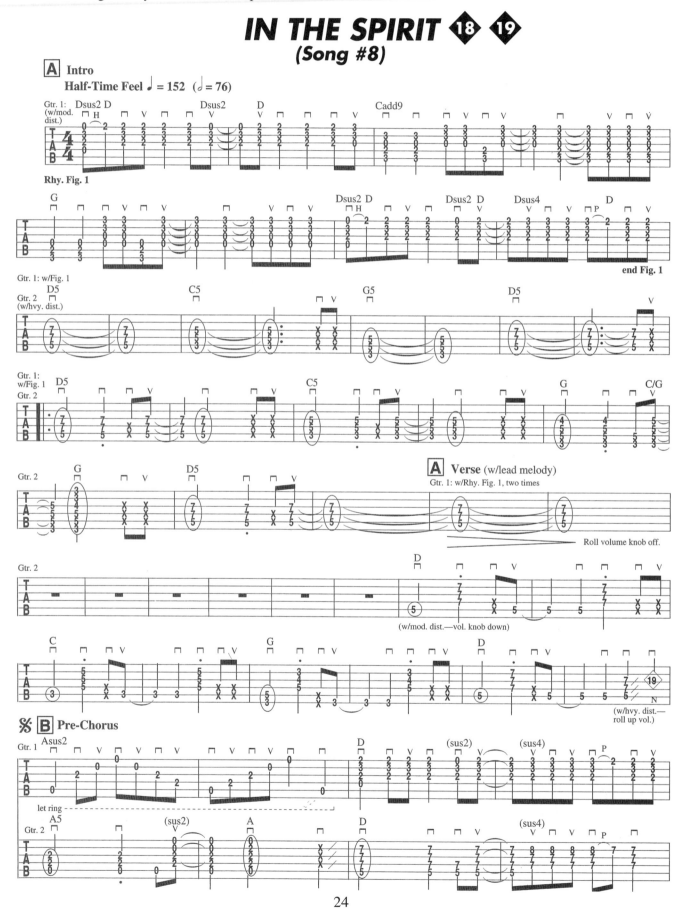

24

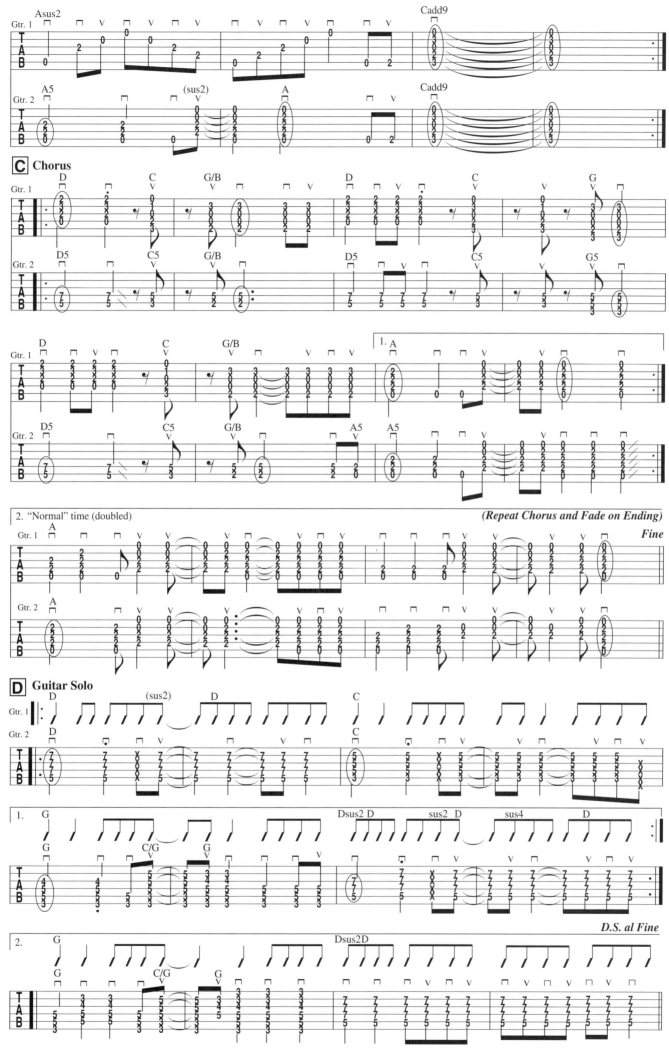

CHAPTER 9

BUILDING CHORDS IN A MINOR KEY

Below, the notes of the E natural minor scale are shown stretched out on a single string. The steps of the scale are numbered 1, 2, ♭3, 4, 5, ♭6, ♭7, showing that this scale uses the same pitches 1, 2, 4, 5 as the parallel major scale (that's E major), but the third, sixth, and seventh steps are flatted one fret. The seven notes found in the key of E minor are E, F♯, G, A, B, C, and D.

E natural minor

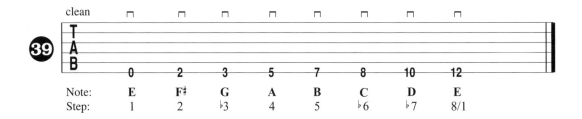

Note:	E	F♯	G	A	B	C	D	E
Step:	1	2	♭3	4	5	♭6	♭7	8/1

Now we'll build chords on each step of this minor scale. So we'll need to *harmonize* it, stacking up intervals of thirds just as we did earlier. But this time, of course, we'll use just the notes of E minor.

Harmonized thirds in key of E minor, as diads

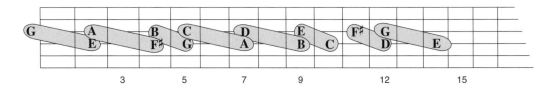

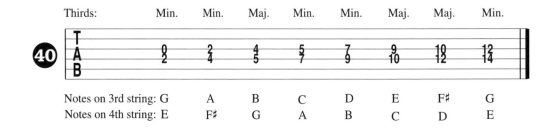

Thirds:	Min.	Min.	Maj.	Min.	Min.	Maj.	Maj.	Min.
Notes on 3rd string:	G	A	B	C	D	E	F♯	G
Notes on 4th string:	E	F♯	G	A	B	C	D	E

Harmonized triads in E minor

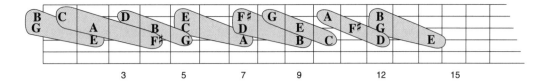

Triad names:	Em	F♯°	G	Am	Bm	C	D	Em

41

```
T  0   1   3   5   7   8   10  12
A  0   2   4   5   7   9   11  12
   2   4   5   7   9   11  12  14
B
```

	Em	F♯°	G	Am	Bm	C	D	Em
2nd string (fifths):	B	C	D	E	F♯	G	A	B
3rd string (thirds):	G	A	B	C	D	E	F♯	G
4th string (roots):	E	F♯	G	A	B	C	D	E

Below are the chords in the key of E minor, in their full barre-chord voicings. The diminished ii chord, however, is altered to a minor chord as this is virtually always the way it appears in practice. As before, roman numerals as used to indicate each chord's relationship to the tonic.

i	ii	♭III	iv	v	♭VI	♭VII	i
Em	*F♯m	G	Am	Bm	C	D	Em

42

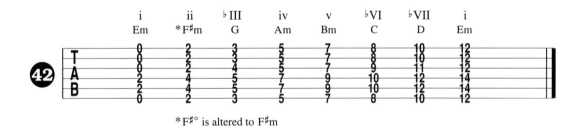

*F♯° is altered to F♯m

TIP: In a minor key, the minor chords are i, iv, v, (and ii, since we've altered it), while the major chords fall on ♭III, ♭VI, and ♭VII. This is good to have memorized.

Note on Relative Major and Minor

Interestingly enough, the sequence of chords in a minor key turns out to be exactly the same as in a major key, except they are displaced. This is because a minor scale can be found lurking within any major scale. Specifically, if you start on the sixth step of a major scale—renumbering it to 1—and play up to the next octave of that note, you will have a natural minor scale. For example, take E major. The sixth step is C♯. So C♯ minor shares the same notes as E major. Scales (and keys) that share the same notes but have different roots, like this, are said to be *related*. See *Metal Lead Guitar Volume 2* for more about using relative major and minor scales and keys.

Several familiar chord progressions are shown below in the key of E minor. See if you can tell which songs they belong to. Play each and write in the correct progression numerals.

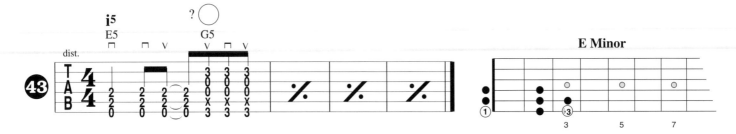

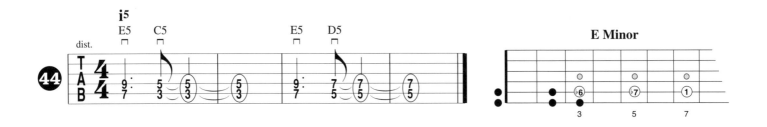

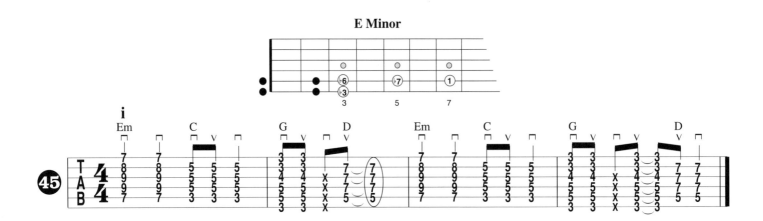

Example 46 is a one bar riff, rather than a progression. In actual progression terms, it basically says "E" with a minor tonality. (Refer to page 9.) Keeping that in mind, though, write in the numerals identifying the chord sequence used by this riff.

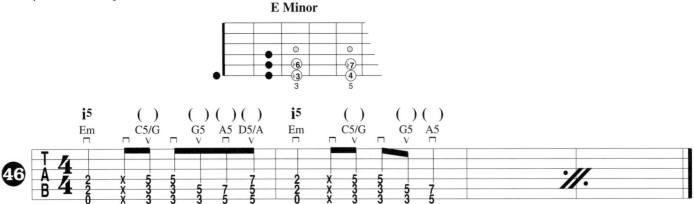

Progressions: Ex. 43, i-♭III; Ex. 44, i5-♭VI5-i5-♭VII5; Ex. 45, i-♭VI-♭III-♭VII;
Ex. 46, i, sequence is i5-♭VI5-♭III5-iv5-♭VII5

Below are the chords in the keys of Gm and Am. Notice that all the chords maintain their same relative position in relation to the new tonic.

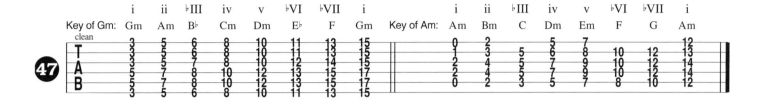

Below are two minor progressions, transposed into Gm and Am. Write in the correct key and progression numerals. Again, the relevant scale patterns are shown underneath each.

G Minor

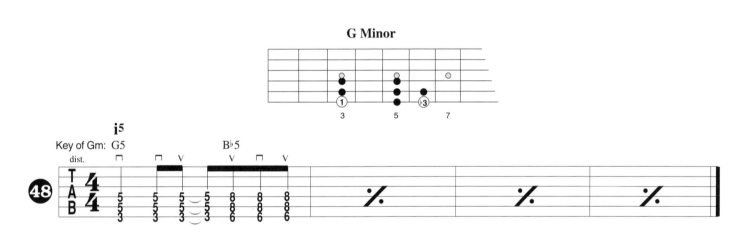

A Minor

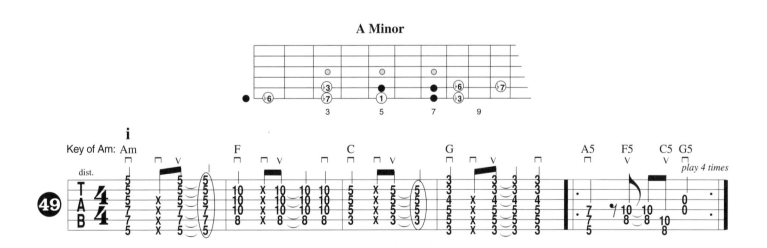

As you've already seen, we routinely alter the ii chord from diminished to minor. Other variations to the harmonized minor scale are also commonplace.

Using a major "V" chord in an otherwise minor key—instead of the naturally occurring minor "v" chord—is often preferred. We can call this alteration a *harmonic minor variation,* because the type of minor scale which does harmonize to a major V chord is called a harmonic minor scale.

> TIP: Note the dominant pull of the major V chord, as it wants to fall to the tonic. The tenseness of the V chord is said to *resolve* to the i chord.

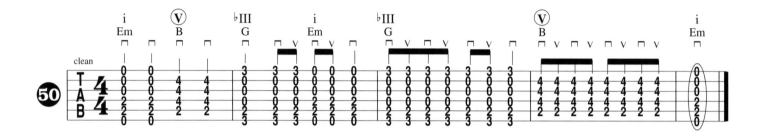

A major "IV" chord in a minor key can likewise be called the *Dorian variation.* The Dorian mode is a type of minor scale that naturally harmonizes to a major IV chord. Note the brightening feel of the major IV chord in the minor progression below.

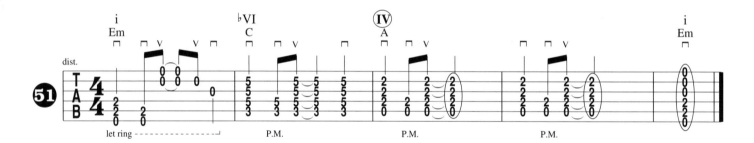

Sometimes even the tonic chord may be altered to major, within a minor key. The riff/progression below, similar to Van Halen's "Unchained," follows a natural minor chord sequence except that in each case, the "i" chord is altered into a major "I" chord. Notice how the feel shifts back and forth between the brightness (on I) and the strong minor quality in the rest of the riff.

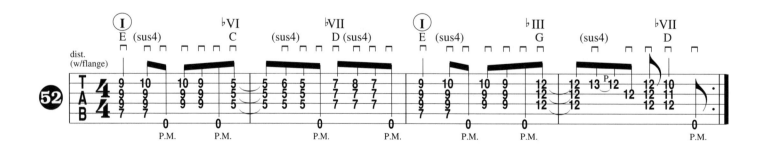

THE ♭V AND ♭II CHORDS ◆24◆

There are two other chord relationships which lie "between the cracks" of the natural minor scale, yet blend nicely with it. Widely incorporated by the original dark metal band Black Sabbath, the ♭V and ♭II have worked their way throughout the metal spectrum, from Metallica, Ministry and Pantera, to Nirvana, Stone Temple Pilots, Alice in Chains, and Slash's Snake Pit, to name just a few bands that draw upon these distinct tonal flavors from time to time.

The ♭V chord goes beyond simply being "dark." It is the *heavy chord*—pure, twisted evil—and imparts a diminished tonality that works well in conjunction with minor keys. It is built upon the ♭5 tone of the blues minor scale, found between 4 and 5. Most often used as a power chord, ♭V harmonizes nicely as a major chord as well. In Em, the ♭V chord is B♭. Notice the relative position and twisted sound of the ♭V in the riff below.

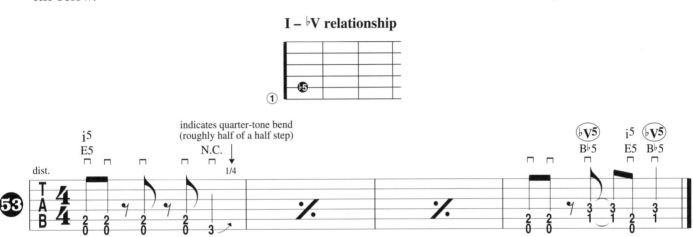

The ♭II chord could be called the *Phrygian variation,* (that's pronounced "frig-e-un"), since the Phrygian mode is a type of minor scale with a flatted, or minor, second step. Again, it is often used as a power chord, but may be harmonized major. In Em, the ♭II chord is F. Notice the characteristic pull of the ♭II in example 54 below, as it wants to fall back to the tonic, similar to the verse riff of "Enter Sandman" by Metallica, but with a different ending tag.

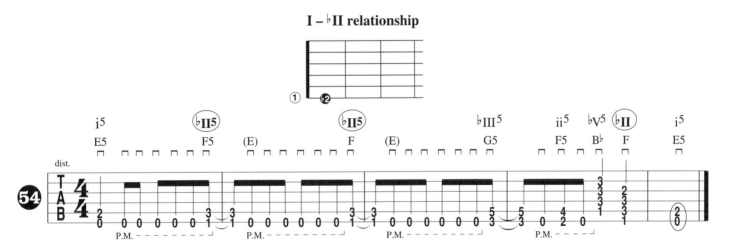

"Blending" keys

These last two pages point toward an important idea in rock and metal—that keys are not exclusive. Songs may blend different types of keys, shifting between major and minor for example. In fact, if you consider all the chords within a major key, its parallel minor key, plus ♭V and ♭II, every possible chromatic tone is covered. So ultimately, once again we see that there are no rules! You can use *any* note or chord, and the resultant "blurring" between keys often creates the most interesting sounds. But it is best to learn major and minor separately first. Then, as you begin to combine them, you will know exactly what you are doing!

31

SIXTEENTH NOTE FIGURES ◆25

You've already tangled with a sixteenth note groove in the last song, "In the Spirit," so this won't be entirely new. The difference is that now we're going to tackle sixteenths head-on, rather than sneaking in through the back door, like we did before.

Sixteenth notes are four notes per beat, or twice as fast as eighth notes. As a general rule, sixteenths are picked with a consistant alternating pattern, with a downstroke on each downbeat.

> TIP: The subdivisions of the beat are often counted "**1**…ee…and…uh…**2**…ee…and…uh…**3**… ee… and…uh…**4**…ee…and…uh."

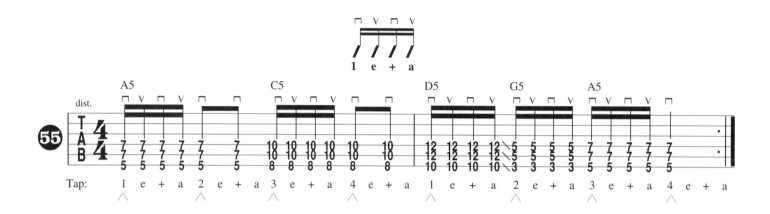

The next two figures combine an eight note and two sixteenths. I call these figures the "gallop" and "reverse gallop."

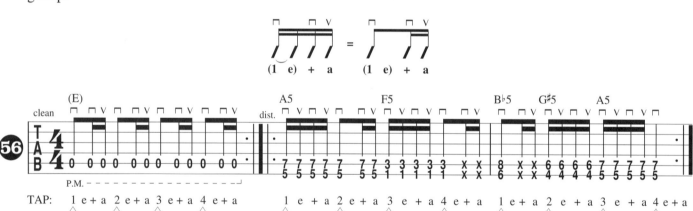

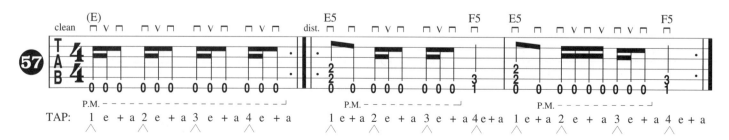

Example 58, below, combines these "gallop" and "reverse gallop" figures in an Ozzy-style, sixteenth note pedal tone riff.

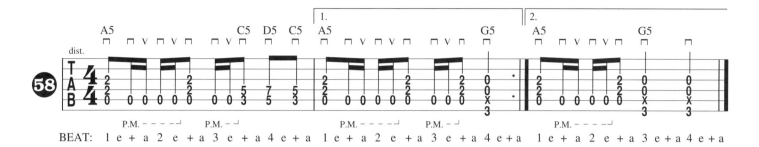

Three sixteenths tied together last three-quarters of a beat. This is written as a dotted eighth note. (A dot placed after a note always adds one-half of the value of that note.) Both possible dotted eighth/sixteenth note figures appear in example 59, a riff/progression in the style of The Offspring's "Self Esteem."

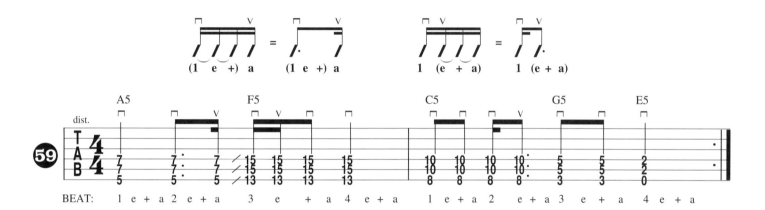

Example 60 uses some more of these dotted eighth/sixteenth figures, in another chordal, sixteenth note strumming approach. Does this progression sound somewhat familiar?

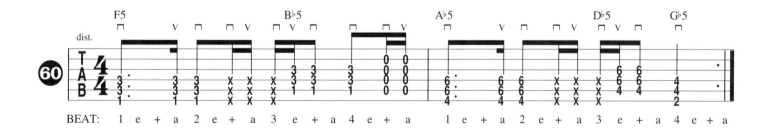

TIP: If you have any trouble with sixteenth note rhythms, try tapping your foot in double time—that is, tap out every eighth note as if it were the underlying beat, rather than the usual quarter note pulse. The effect will be that sixteenth note rhythms are instantly transformed into eighth note rhythms (at double tempo). When you can play it that way, in eighths, then try dropping back into half time to play it with a sixteenth note groove.

POWER CHORD EXTENSIONS 26

Power chords can be rooted on strings other than the low E and A strings. Here, we will look at power chords rooted on the D and G strings. These power chords can be thought of as extensions, as I will explain in a moment.

Power chords rooted on the fourth, or D string, are a moveable form of the open D power chord. As such, they may be played as either a two-note diad, or in their fuller, three-string shape.

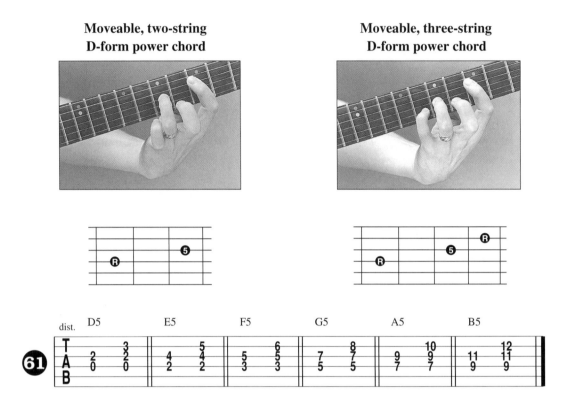

The fifth of the chord shape is sometimes added underneath the root, to give a fuller sound. Technically, the result is a second inversion slash chord. Example 62, below, uses this second inversion chord in a riff reminiscent of Foo Fighters' "I'll Stick Around."

TIP: Each D-form power chord is connected to an E-form shape that you already know, as shown below. Use this extension system to help you find the correct positions for these D string power chords.

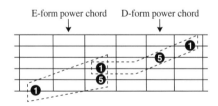

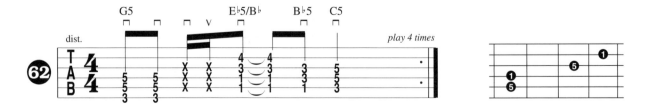

Now let's take a look at the power chords rooted on the third, or G, string. These are a moveable form of the partial open G power chord. They are shown below in the three-string version, and in the four-string, slash-chord version (with the fifth in the bass).

Moveable, three-string G-form power chord

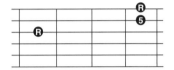

Moveable, four-string G-form power chord

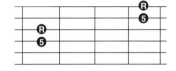

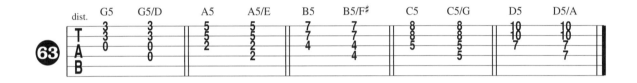

TIP: Each G-form power chord is an extension of the A-form power chord, rooted on the fifth string (just as the D-form was an extension of the E-form power chord). The diagram below illustrates.

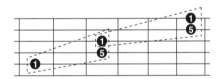

The following riff uses all four moveable power chord shapes. Practice it until you can form each chord shape quickly, without hesitation.

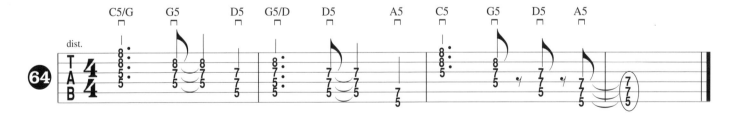

TIP: Experiment with these alternate power chord shapes. You may substitute them into any riff or progression in place of the standard E- and A-form power chords.

35

"Nervosa" is a moderately upbeat Nirvana/Offspring-type grunge-pop-punk groove with a driving chordal approach in sixteenths. Notice the natural harmonic mutes as well as the stylistically characteristic changes in dynamics within the verses. The overall song form is chorus(as intro)/verse/chorus/transition riff/verse/chorus/transition riff/solo/chorus, or A-BAC-BAC-D-AA.

The key is Am. Write in the correct progression numerals throughout. Hint: In the key of A, the ♭II chord is B♭, the ♭V chord is E♭.

NERVOSA ◆27◆ ◆28◆
(Song #9)

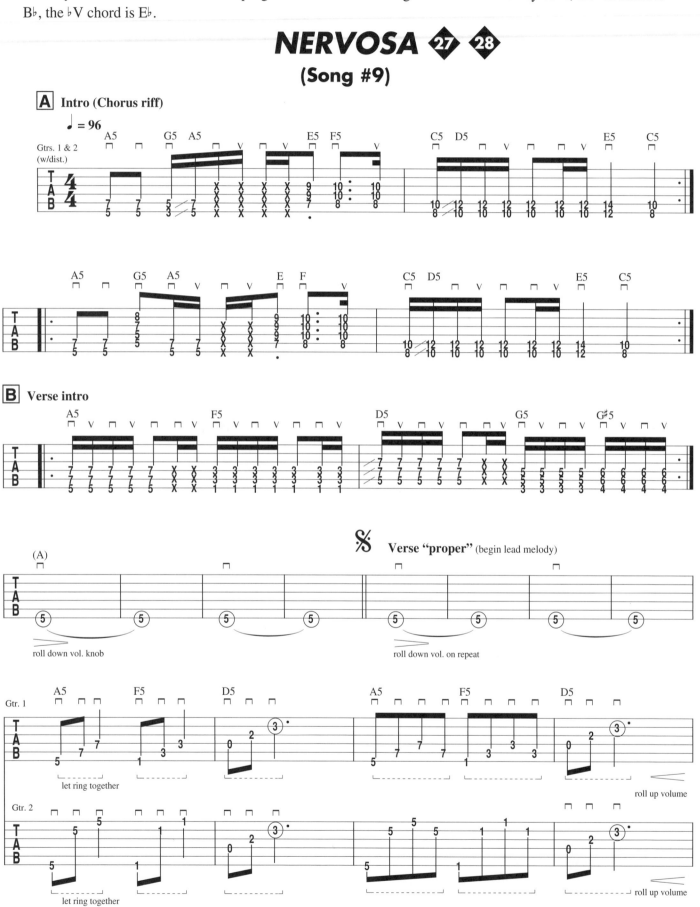

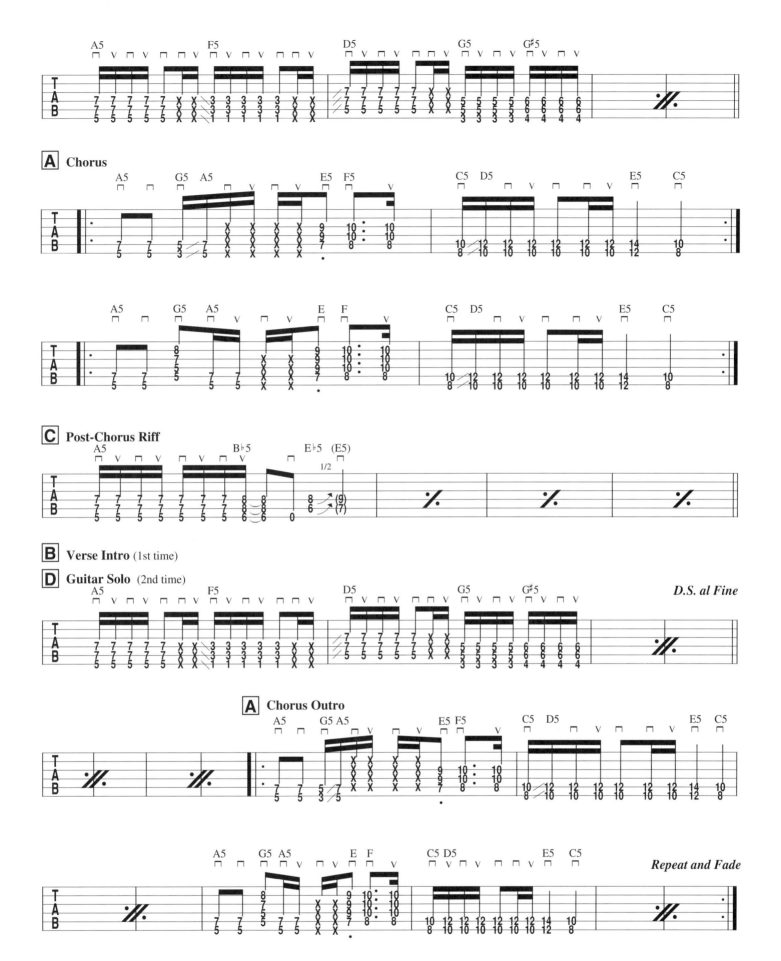

Now go back to *Volume 1* as well as the first chapter here in *Volume 2,* and write in the key and chord numerals for every progression and riff. And remember all the relative patterns. Sound like a lot of work? Well, when you finish with that, I guarantee you'll have a good handle on this stuff. And that's the idea! You should know this stuff like the back of your own hand. No! You should know it better than that!!

CHAPTER 10

SIXTEENTH NOTE "OFFBEAT" ACCENTS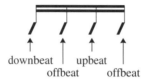

The figure below points out the terminology commonly used to describe the different portions of a beat, when subdivided into sixteenths. As you already know, the *downbeat* refers to the beginning point of the beat itself while the term *upbeat* refers to the halfway point between downbeats, represented by the "&." The other portions of a beat are commonly referred to as *offbeats*. So within a sixteenth note figure, the second and fourth sixteenths are offbeats.

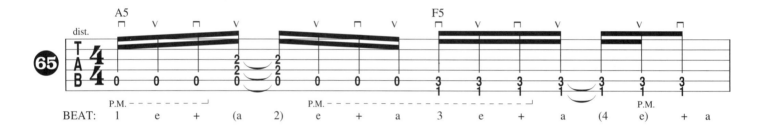

The following rhythm places accents on these sixteenth note offbeats. Remember, you need to keep your foot tapping out the beat steadily. Otherwise, you won't get the true feel of the rhythm.

> TIP: Count the portions of the beat—"1…ee…&…uh…2…ee…&…uh…"—as you play. That will help you feel the underlying subdivisions consistently and keep your rhythms in time.

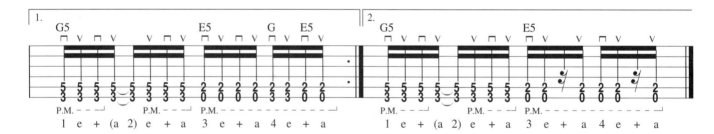

When an eighth note is sandwiched between two sixteenths, it creates an interesting offbeat syncopation. Example 66 gives a White Zombie-style syncopated rhythm in E. Another good example which relies heavily upon this same sixteenth/eighth/sixteenth figure is the riff from Led Zepplin's "Immigrant Song."

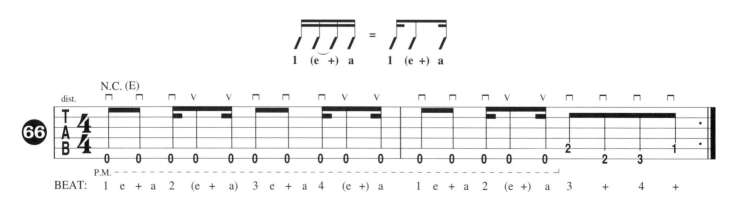

RHYTHMIC PATTERNS IN SIXTEENTHS ◈30

As you already know, *rhythmic patterns* occur whenever a sequence of notes is repeated over a different rhythmic grouping. Earlier we saw a three note sequence repeated over eighth notes. Here we'll try them in sixteenths.

Notice how the three note sequence below "turns around the beat," first beginning on a downbeat then falling on the fourth sixteenth, the upbeat, the second sixteenth, and finally rejoining the downbeat.

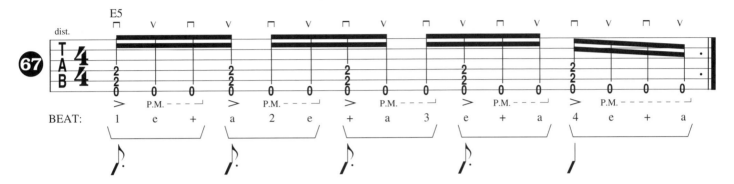

Just as before, the three "note" sequence can include rests or ties. Listen for the same rhythmic effect in the phrase below.

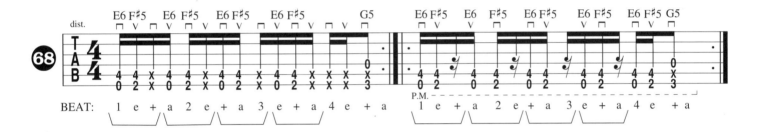

The same rhythm you heard above as example 67 is hiding within both halves of the phrase below. However, when we add ties (in the second half), this interesting offbeat rhythm emerges.

> TIP: This is probably the single most common, offbeat metal rhythm. Listen for it in songs that you hear.

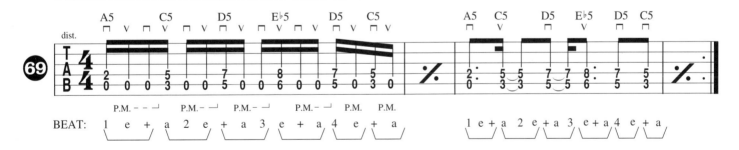

Finally, let's try a set of six over sixteenths. Specifically, we'll make it five notes and a rest. Although it's essentially just a one note riff (with an ending tag), the rhythmic pattern effect makes it sound cool.

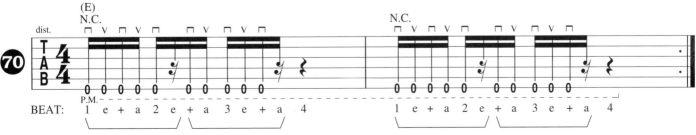

39

So far, we have used alternating picking for all sixteenth note rhythms. This is most often the case, but sometimes you may want to play sixteenth note figures with an all downstroke approach. Remember, it gives a somewhat heavier and more intense feel that is especially effective with palm muting. But how fast can one do downstroke picking? Hmmm….I don't seem to recall seeing any speed limits around here…

Practice the following rhythms as speed exercises. Play along to a metronome and gradually increase your tempo until you can't push it up any more. Each is played twice on the track, first slow then fast. See if eventually you can build up your speed to match the tempo played in the faster versions. Good luck!

TIP: Distance equals time. So smaller motions of the pick will enable you to go faster. Try to avoid tensing up too much.

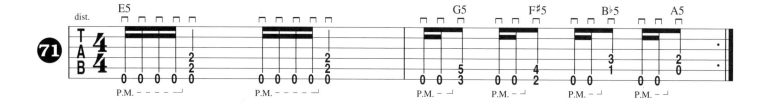

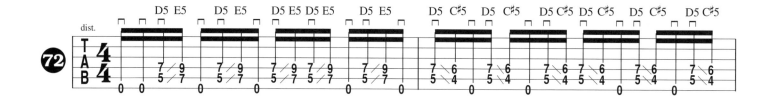

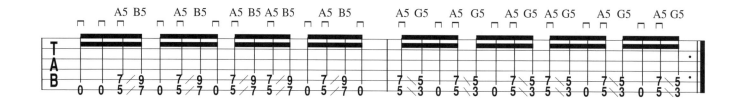

Accent picking is a hybrid between alternate picking and downstroke picking. Here we will use downstroke picking as our basic approach, and we will add upstrokes—not in a strumming format—but simply to help accent certain notes and/or chords.

> TIP: Striking a chord from the top—with an upstroke rather than a downstroke—will tend to favor the higher-sounding strings and therefore make the chords stand out more from surrounding palm mutes.

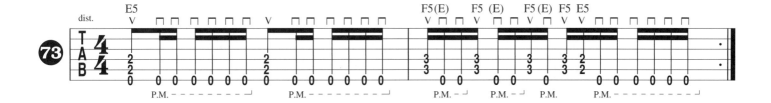

It's not a huge difference. But it is a difference nonetheless. And it's a difference you can exploit. The next riff blends some downstroke and alternating picking to accent several back to back upbeats.

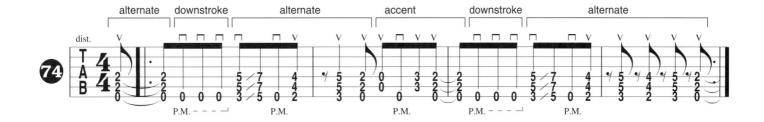

> TIP: This frees you from using just one picking format. Really, you can hit the strings however you want. As long as you have the groove, it doesn't really matter. Hey, what was that rule again? *There are no rules!!!*

MORE BARRE CHORD SHAPES ◆32◆

In chapter seven, we made full major and minor barre chords using the open E and open A shapes. Now, let's take a look at barring up the other three open chord shapes—D, G, and C. And then we'll see how all of the shapes are interconnected on the fretboard.

The D-form major and minor barre chords are similar to the D-form moveable power chords—just with an added major 3rd or minor 3rd chord tone.

D-form, major barre chord

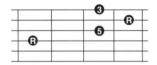

D-form, minor barre chord

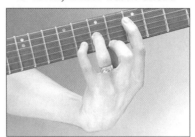

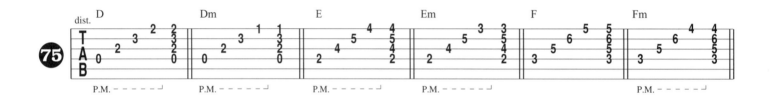

Although playable, the major shape shown above is a bit inconvenient. Below, a more comfortable, partial shape of the D form barre-chord is shown.

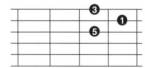

Example 76 uses this partial D-form barre chord together with an open D string pedal tone, in an upbeat folk-influenced rock style.

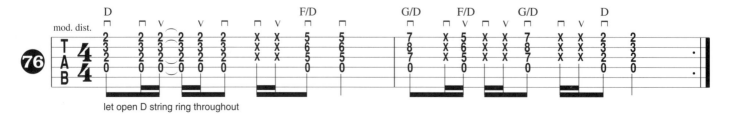

let open D string ring throughout

Now let's look at the open C shape. The full, moveable C-form barre chord shape is shown below.

C-form, major barre chord

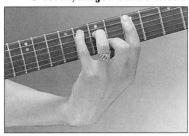

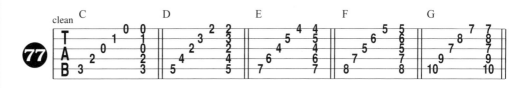

The C-form barre chord is also more commonly played using a partial shape. Example 78 demonstrates the partial shape below in a riff. Notice its easy accessibility from the partial A major form, and its almost cliché rock sound. Does this bring any songs to mind?

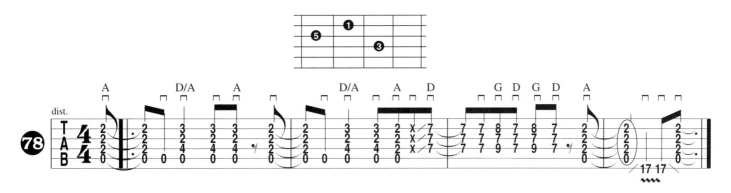

Finally, we arrive at the open G shape. Here is the full, moveable G-form barre chord. It's a bear.

G-form, major barre chord

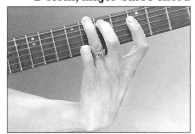

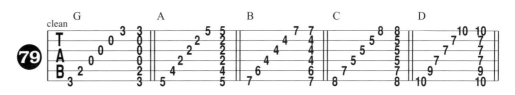

Again, the whole G-form barre chord is somewhat difficult to fret, but pieces of it are commonly used. The partial barre chord shape below is a first inversion chord, with the third in the bass. Example 80 is reminiscent of the Stone Temple Pilots' "Interstate Love Song."

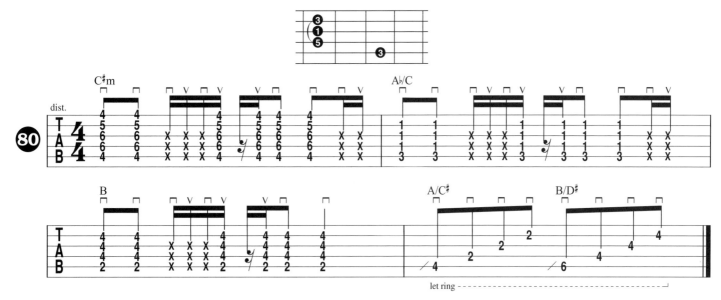

43

Now that you know the five main barre chord shapes, we will look at how they intertwine to cover the entire fretboard. All five forms of E major are shown below. Play each shape one after another.

> TIP: As you are fretting each chord, visualize the connecting shapes both above and below the one you are actually playing at that moment. This will help you begin to see them all together at once.

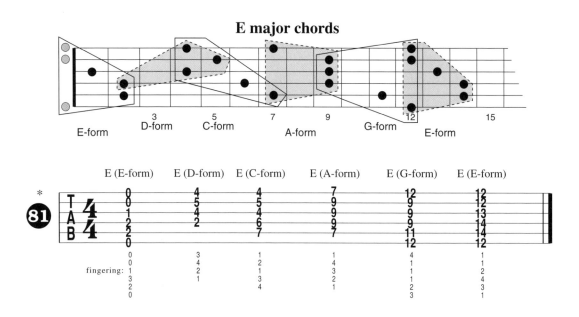

Below are the five forms of A major. The sequence of shape connections stays intact. Only the positioning of the entire pattern moves.

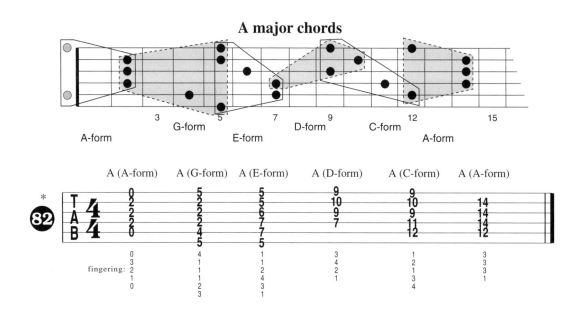

> TIP: Knowing this pattern of "interconnectedness" will help you immensely when you begin to learn lead guitar scale shapes. So learn it well!

*omitted from recording.

Artificial harmonics are also known as pick harmonics, pinch harmonics, or false harmonics, because they are created with a sort of "pinching" technique of the picking hand, quite distinct from the technique used to create so-called "natural" harmonics. However, the effect is similar, in that they create a higher pitched harmonic in place of the normal sounding tone of the note.

Listen to guitarist Zakk Wylde in "Coming Home" or "No More Tears" (Ozzy Osbourne), for some excellent examples of these artificial, or pinch harmonics. The technique is not complicated, but it does take a little practice to execute it just when you want it. Here's how it works:

Pick the string at the same time that you are lightly touching it with the fleshy part of your thumb (or any other finger). This creates the harmonic by not allowing the string to vibrate its full length normally. Different pitches will be produced depending on exactly where you touch the string as you pick. But here we will not worry about the exact pitches because it really doesn't matter. We are after the general effect.

TIP: After picking the string, move your thumb (or finger) away immediately so the string is not deadened.

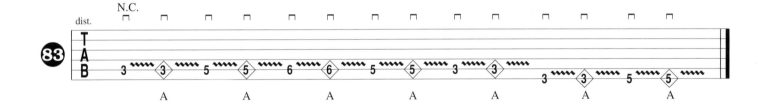

Practice creating artificial harmonics is the riff below. They are particularly attention-getting when combined with a smooth, wide finger vibrato. (Also, note the Ozzy-style, ballad feel here.)

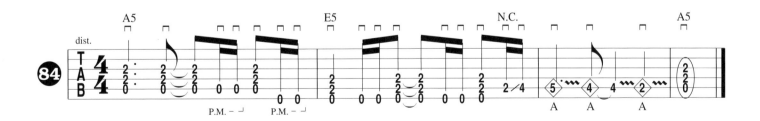

SEVENTH AND NINTH CHORDS ◆35◆

Seventh and ninth chords are definitely less common in metal, but they do sometimes make an appearance so we'll take a brief look at them. Seventh chords tend to give a bluesy feel because of their strong association with that style of music. Ninth chords give a more jazzy feel because of their association with that style. To hear these chords at work in a metal and rock context, listen to "Rest in Peace," by Extreme, "Rock and Roll is Dead," by Lenny Kravitz, or Pearl Jam's "Escape." They are also quite common in the alternative funk rock style of the Red Hot Chili Peppers.

Seventh chords are formed by adding another third interval on top of the fifth tone. There are three types of seventh chords we will look at here are dominant 7th, minor 7th, and major 7th.

The dominant 7th type is the most common. So much so, in fact, that it is generally called just a "7th" chord for short. The chord tones for a dominant 7th are 1, 3, 5, ♭7, so you can see that its a major chord with an added ♭7. Several common dominant 7th shapes are shown below. Each of these shapes is also "barred up" the neck in example 85.

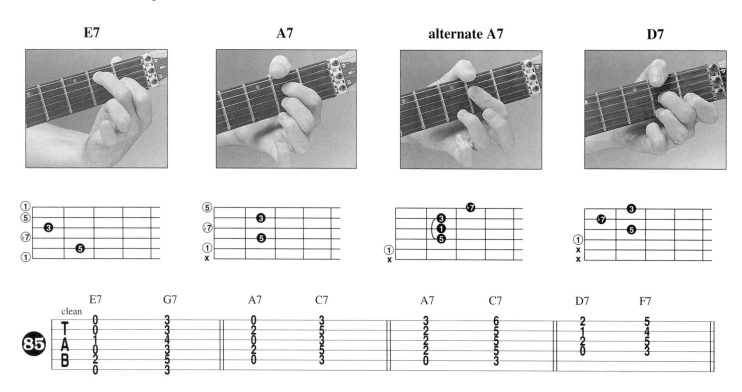

Notice the distinct flavor of the dominant 7th chord in the ending tag of the following single note riff, à la Lenny Kravitz.

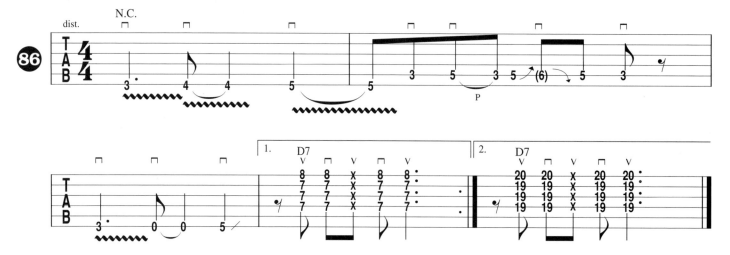

46

A *minor 7th* is a minor chord with an added ♭7. So the formula for a minor 7th is 1, ♭3, 5, ♭7. On the other hand, a *major 7th* is a major chord with an added major 7th, or 1, 3, 5, 7. Below are some common minor and major 7th shapes. Each is "barred up" the neck in example 87.

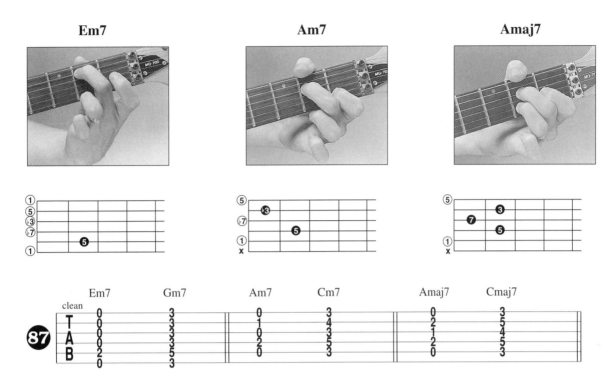

A ninth chord is formed by stacking yet another third on top of the seventh. There are even more varieties of ninths, but we'll just look at two—the standard 9th chord and an augmented 9th. The standard *9th chord* is simply a dominant seventh with the added ninth tone. The *augmented 9th,* or 7♯9, is the famous "Purple Haze" chord, pioneered by proto-heavy metal guitarist, Jimi Hendrix. Note the tenseness of this unusual-sounding chord. Below are some common barre chord shapes for the 9th and augmented 9th chords, followed by a riff which applies them both.

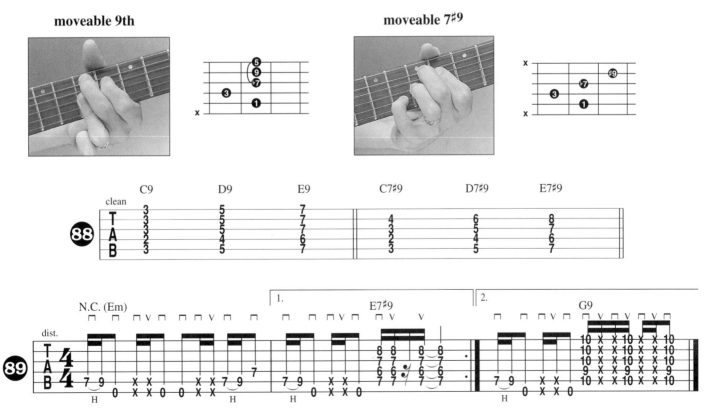

47

UN-COMMON TIME ◆36

The 4/4 time signature actually spells out just what it is. The top number indicates that there are four beats per measure, while the bottom number tells you that a quarter note receives one beat. This is by far the most common time signature—in fact, it's even called *common time*. But sometimes, riffs are created that intentionally form measures of other lengths, such as three, five, six, or seven beats.

The time signature of 5/4 has five beats per measure, with a quarter note still getting one full beat. Listen to Soundgarden's "My Wave" for a good example of a song that uses 5/4 time. The riff below, shown as example 90, is also in 5/4 time.

> TIP: Notice how the drums support the 5/4 time, repeating the pattern in each five beat repetition.

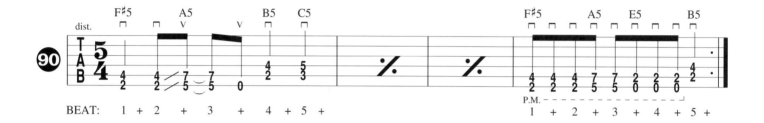

The riff below falls into 6/4 time. Of course it could be written in 4/4, (lasting one and one-half measures before it repeats), but 6/4 is a more accurate way to represent it. This time signature coincides perfectly with a straight 4/4 drumbeat, but nevertheless, the phrase length still feels a bit odd.

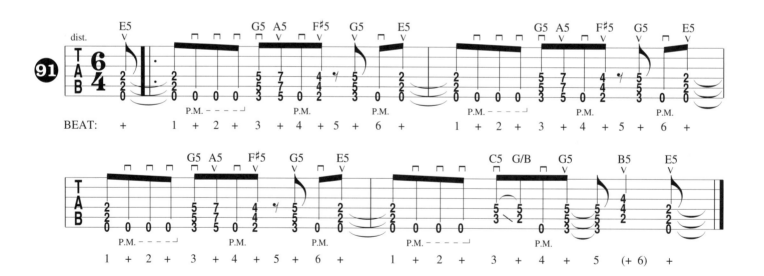

For some examples of 6/4 time, listen to "Black Hole Sun," by Soundgarden, and check out "As Darkness Gathers," back in Volume 1, chapter six. The solo riff is written in 4/4, but it is truly 6/4.

The time signature of 7/4 is another oddity, leaving you with the distinct impression that something is missing. Indeed, it is. One beat has been left out of each two-measure, 4/4 phrase. Sometimes 7/4 is written as one measure of 4/4 and one measure of 3/4, alternating. Whatever. It's the same thing. Songs using 7/4 time include Soundgarden's "Spoonman" and "Outshined."

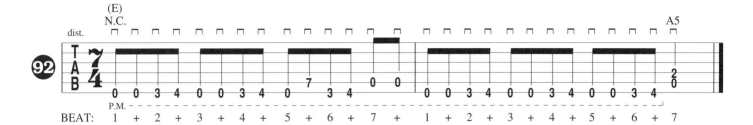

Now just when you thought is was safe to go back and resume 4/4-ing, things get really weird—with 7/8 time. Technically, an eighth note on the bottom means that it gets one full beat (like a normal quarter note). This gives the impression that 7/8 may simply be another way of writing 7/4 time. But that would be silly. What's the point? No, this time signature is 4/4 time minus *one half* a beat. The eighth note count is really a double time count. For a few examples of 7/8 time at work, listen to Led Zepplin's "The Ocean," Rush's "Tom Sawyer," or Alice in Chains' "Them Bones."

Listen to the riff below and notice how the drums draw you into a basic 4/4 feel, then suddenly you lose it! Count double time, on the eighth notes though, and you'll see seven beats and repeat. Pretty cool, huh?

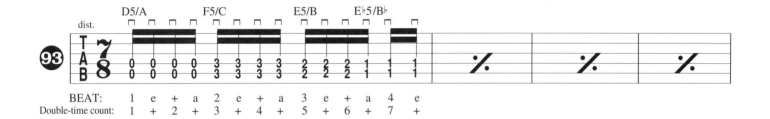

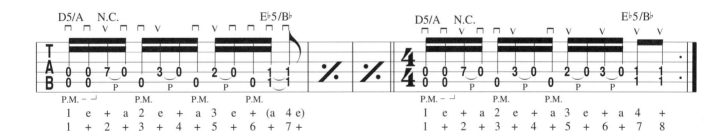

It is possible to continue down this path to a level of complete bizarreness and complexity that just about no one can anticipate. Listen to a Dream Theater CD, for example. One word of warning, though—you better put some practice time in if you want to do 7/16 time, or it's going to become a big mess real fast! But it maybe an interesting mess, nonetheless. Who knows?

"MonsterFunker" is the tenth song of the method, featuring a funk/rap metal style with some severely offbeat funk rhythms à la Rage Against the Machine, or the Red Hot Chili Peppers. The intro starts with a military-type snare drum cadence and a flip-flopping major/minor progression in A. But this is soon shattered by the heavy chorus riff, punching out the F#m blues scale, replete with tense ♭5-to-5 bends. The bridge incorporates 6/4 time. Count, or you may miss it! Later, in the solo interlude, seventh and ninth chords appear. Then along comes a temporary return to the bright expanse of A major. The overall form is intro/chorus/verse/chorus/verse/chorus/bridge/solo/respite(that's the part in A major)/chorus, or: A-B-CB-CB-DEF-B. Definitely a motherfunking monsterfuncker.

MONSTERFUNKER 37 38
(Song #10)

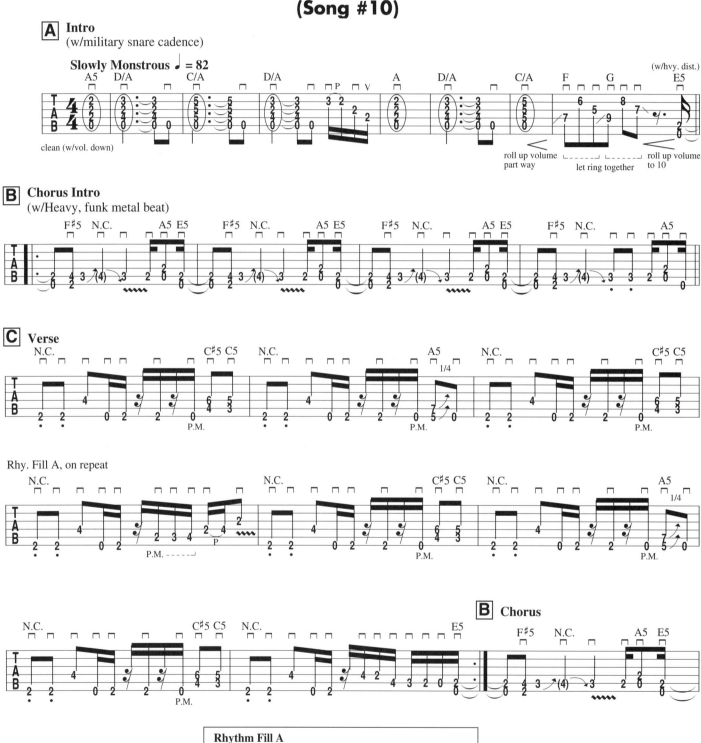

50

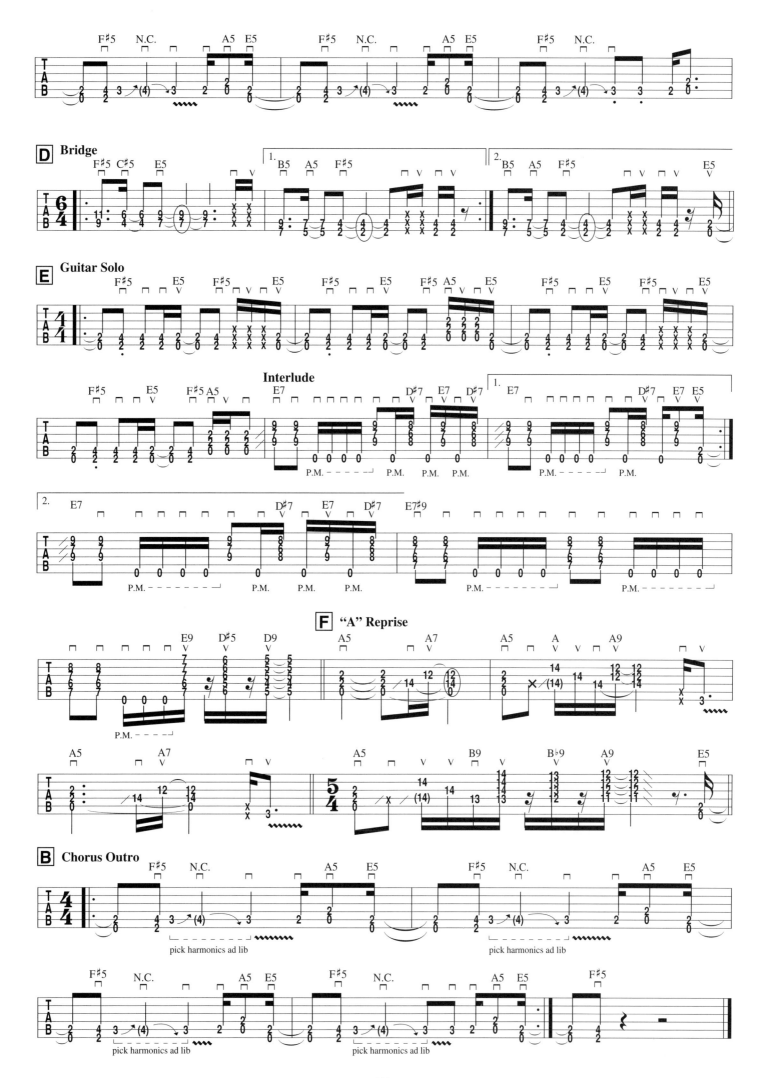

51

CHAPTER 11

MORE DIAD SHAPES ⟨39⟩

When you were formally introduced to diads back in Volume 1, chapter 4, you learned about fifth and fourth diads, and how their shapes may be found with in the expanded power chord shape. You were also shown major sixth and minor seventh diads in the context of comping figures, later in that same chapter. Then in Volume 2, chapter 8, you saw major and minor third diads as we harmonized the major and minor scales, and you learned about using a minor sixth diad as a first inversion major chord. Now, we're going to bring all the diads together for a little diad reunion. But first, I have to introduce the stragglers.

Octaves

The octave diad has no doubt already been glimpsed by many of you, as the octave concept was first pointed out way back in Volume 1, chapter 2. But we never actually played it as a diad until now. Make sure the string that lies between is muted well, so it won't sound by accident. Notice its relatively thin sound.

Moveable octave diad

Diminished fifths

The diminished fifth diad shouldn't look too surprising. It's the shape that the roots in a I-♭V-I chord relationship make. It is also known as the *tritone,* because it spans a distance of three (tri-) whole steps (-tone). When played as a chord diad, it gives us a harsh *dissonance.* That is, the notes do not blend together nicely, but rather, they sound turbulent and unsettled.

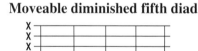

Moveable diminished fifth diad

Major sevenths

The major seventh diad is one fret less than the octave. It is also a dissonant interval. Although somewhat rare in metal, the major seventh diad has been known to make an occasional appearance. (Look at the beginning of Metallica's "One," for example.)

Moveable major seventh diad

Major and minor seconds

Second diads are also rare, but never say never. Any set of notes can work, it's just a matter of how it is done. Another clear set of dissonances, a major second is an interval of a whole step, or two frets, while a minor second is an interval of a half-step, or one fret.

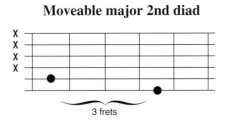

Moveable major 2nd diad

3 frets

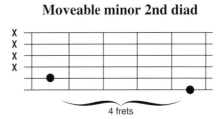

Moveable minor 2nd diad

4 frets

Now let's line them all up in a row, and get some structure in here. You can see that every half step between the octave A's has been accounted for.

Diads based on "A":

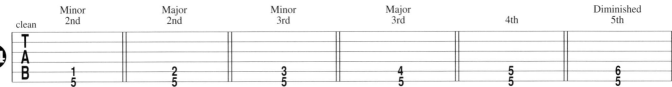

The following riff uses several different diad shapes. Play it, then write in the correct name above each diad. The answers are given below.

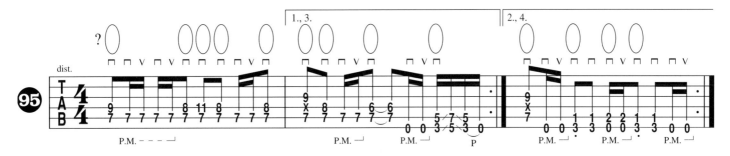

Answers: 5th, dim 5th, maj 6th, dim 5th, dim 5th; oct, dim 5th, maj 3rd, 5th; oct, min 3rd, 5th, min 3rd.

TRIPLETS 40

A *triplet* is three notes which are evenly spaced within the time of two. So *eighth note triplets* are three notes spaced evenly within the time normally occupied by two eighth notes, which is one full beat. Notice the small "3" above each of the rhythmic figures below, indicating they are triplets.

> TIP: Triplet subdivisions can be counted using the syllables "1…trip-…let…2…trip-…let…3…trip-…let…4…trip-…let."

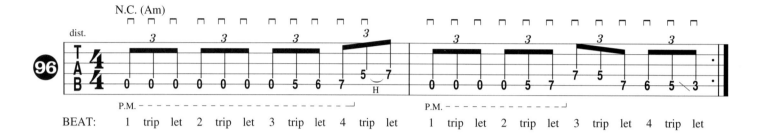

Example 97 mixes straight eighth notes with triplet fills.

> TIP: Switching between the "**1**…&…**2**…&…"-feel and the "**1**…trip-…let…**2**…trip-…let…"-feel can be a little tricky to get. Listen to it a few times. Then try tapping out the rhythm as you follow along. When you can do that, you are ready to play it.

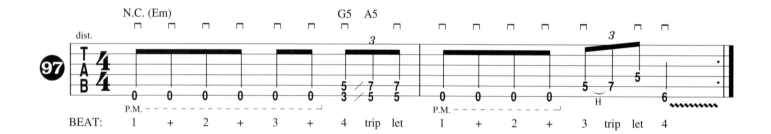

The single-note riff below blends sixteenth note figures with eighth note triplets. Keep your beat even and steady.

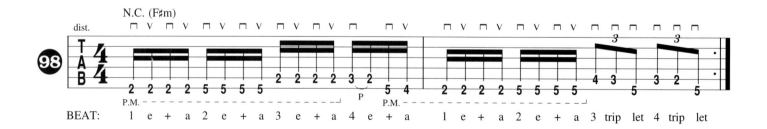

54

Sixteenth note triplets are three notes evenly spaced within the time normally occupied by two sixteenths, or a half beat. Alternating picking is often necessary to play these faster sixteenth triplet rhythms, as in the Metallica/Sepultura-inspired riff below.

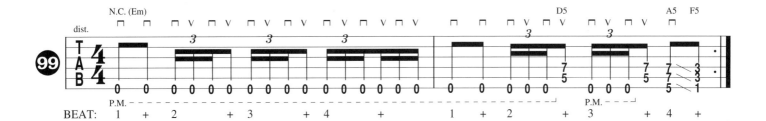

12/8 AND SHUFFLE RHYTHMS 41

When triplets are the basis of the groove, rather than the exception, the song will often be written in 12/8 time. Songs in 12/8 time, for example, include "For Whom the Bell Tolls" by Metallica, "Psycho Holiday" by Pantera, "Simple Lessons," by Candlebox, and "Release" by Pearl Jam.

Technically, in 12/8 time there are twelve beats per measure, and an eighth note gets one beat. But it is always played in its "cut time" version, with four main beats per measure and each main beat subdivided into three "sub-beats."

What does this really mean? It means that 12/8 is just like 4/4, but instead of dividing the beat into halves, here the pulse naturally subdivides into triplets. Therefore, triplet brackets are unnecessary in 12/8.

Simple enough, right? There's just one other thing you need to know. Now, *three* eighth notes add up to one full, compound beat. So a quarter note in 4/4 time equals a *dotted quarter note* in 12/8 time.

55

Example 100 uses a 12/8 groove. Remember, the rules have changed. Now a *dotted* quarter note—the equivalent of *three* tied eighth notes—gets one full beat.

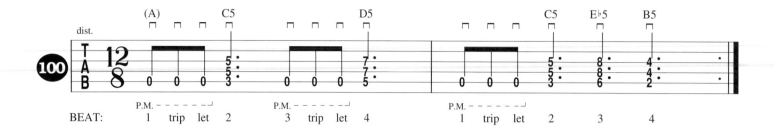

A shuffle rhythm, or swing rhythm, occurs when the first two notes of each triplet group are tied. This is written as a quarter-eighth figure.

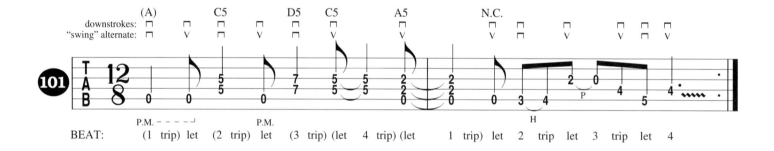

Listen to the characteristic shuffle feel in example 101. The triplet fills blend right into it, since both are based on the same triplet pulse. First, try picking all downstrokes, then try the "swing" alternate picking.

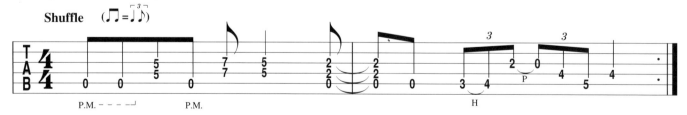

Shuffle rhythms are also often written in 4/4 time as straight eighth notes, with the indication at the beginning—"shuffle: ♫ = ♩♪." This means to "swing" the eighth notes, playing straight eighth notes as if they were written as a shuffle. Example 101 is rewritten below using this format.

Example 101 rewritten, "shorthand":

QUARTER NOTE TRIPLETS 42

Quarter note triplets are three notes evenly spaced over two beats. Although slower, they are actually more difficult to play because of their offbeat, staggered feel.

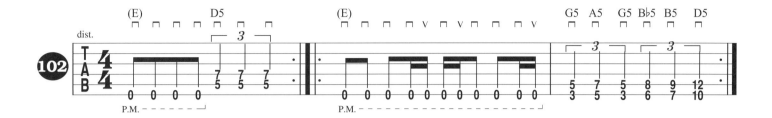

That seems pretty tough to get the right feel, doesn't it? It need not be, if we break it down. First, we'll start with a triplet-based "rhythmic pattern," and work back up. We will use a two-note pattern against triplets.

> TIP: In the second measure, feel the subdivision of each tied note *as if* you were playing it. But of course, miss the string and don't actually pick it. That way, the time location of each tied note is clear.

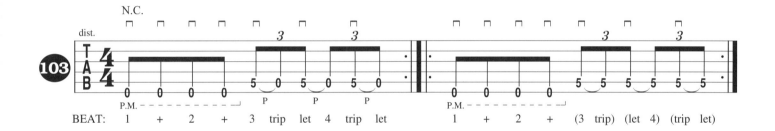

That's it! You just played quarter note triplets. See, each group of two tied eighth notes can be rewritten as a quarter note, and we have exactly the same thing as in the first measure of example 103, above. The difference is that now you know how to feel the hidden triplet subdivisions, and the mystery is solved. So from now on, every time you see quarter note triplets, think of them as you did in example 103 and they'll trouble you no more.

Finally, let's consider quarter note triplets in 12/8 time. Remember, in 12/8, a dotted quarter note gets one full beat—not a regular quarter note. So three back-to-back quarter notes actually make a quarter note triplet. Again, the triplet brackets are simply left off when we shift from 4/4 into 12/8. Actually, feeling quarter note triplets in 12/8 should be a bit easier, because the underlying pulse of triplets is there throughout, unlike in the examples above. On the other hand, there is a little syncopation surprise waiting for you in example 104.

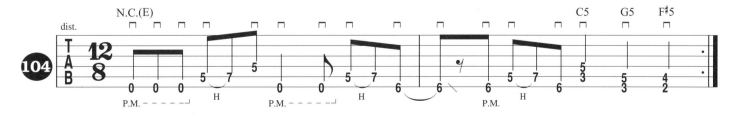

DROPPED D TUNING ◆43

Dropped D tuning is a common alternate tuning used in metal. Songs played in Dropped D include "Black Hole Sun" by Soundgarden, "Go" by Pearl Jam, and "Shine" by Collective Soul, just to name a few. By making the sixth string a low D, not only is the pitch lower, but the string tends to flap around a bit more. The result is a deeper, heavier sound.

For dropped D tuning, the sixth string, or low E string is lowered a whole step to D. All the other strings remain unchanged. One good method of accomplishing this is to hit the fourth D string and the low E string together, then lower the E string until the octaves of D sound in tune:

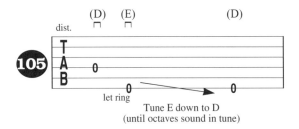

Good. You are in dropped D tuning. The open strings are now D, A, D, G, B, E. Let's take a look around. First of all, the names of the notes on the sixth string have all shifted up two frets. The open sixth string is now D, the second fret is E, third is F, fifth is now G, etc.

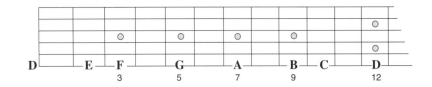

The single note riff below uses dropped D tuning. Notice the deeper tone.

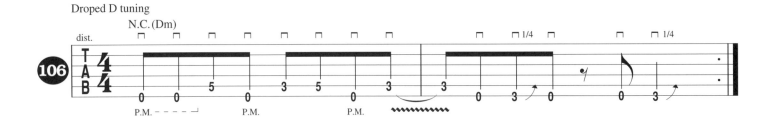

Since you have to raise a note up two frets in order to maintain its original pitch, the power chord shape rooted on the sixth string must be changed to account for this.

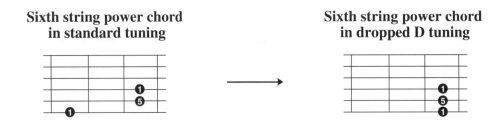

Sixth string power chord in standard tuning   Sixth string power chord in dropped D tuning

Dropped D is gnarly!

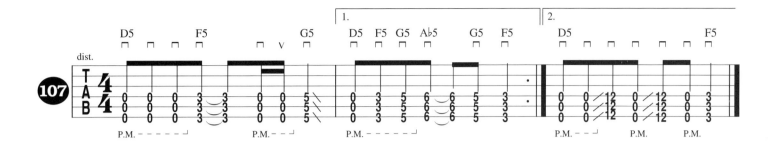

OTHER TUNINGS

E♭ Tuning

Rock and metal bands often tune each string down a half step, thereby lowering everything across the board. This is known as *E♭ tuning*, and it is probably even more common than standard tuning. Technically, every note will produce the absolute pitch one half step lower. So the open strings are E♭, A♭, D♭, G♭, B♭, E♭. However, we do not change the name of any of the notes or chords on the fretboard. We still call an open E chord, and "E" chord. We simply add the caveat that we are in E♭ tuning. Songs recorded in E♭ tuning include most Van Halen, Kiss, Ozzy Osbourne, Jimi Hendrix, Stevie Ray Vaughan, Alice in Chains, and Guns 'N' Roses, just to point out a few examples.

E♭-dropped-D Tuning

If we start with E♭ tuning and lower the sixth string another whole step, as in dropped D tuning, we have *E♭- dropped-D tuning*. Now we're really getting down there. Although technically, the low sixth string would register as a D♭/C♯ on an electronic tuner, we would again simply refer to it as a "D" note, knowing that in absolute terms, everything is really a half step lower. Again, for terminology purposes, we would not change the note names on the fretboard from those of standard dropped D tuning. Some songs recorded in E♭-dropped-D tuning include "No More Tears" by Ozzy Osbourne, and Nirvana's "Heart-Shaped Box," among others.

D Tuning and C♯ Tuning

If all the strings are lowered across the board one whole step below standard E tuning, we have *D tuning*. Of course this is just like E♭ tuning, but a half step lower. C♯ tuning is just dropped one more half step, so each string is lowered one and a half steps (the equivalent of three frets) below standard tuning. This ultra-heavy tuning was explored by Black Sabbath in the early 70's, and today has been revisited and experimented with by bands like Soundgarden and White Zombie. Listen, for example, to White Zombie's "More Human than Human" for a good case in point. By the way, in case you are wondering, actually any pitch can become the tuning standard. You could for example tune half way between E and E♭, and as long as every instrument is tuned the same, no problems will arise.

Open and Alternate Tunings

Open G tuning, consisting of the open string pitches D, G, D, G, B, D is a common tuning used to play slide guitar. Other open tunings and various alternate tunings are also used by different groups from time to time. Soundgarden, for example, is quite adventurous in terms of unusual tunings. The song "My Wave," for example utilizes the pitches E, E (octave), B, B, B, B (octave). By experimenting with new and different tunings, new musical life may be found within old patterns. The down side is that you either need a lot of different guitars, or a lot of patience—having to retune to play every song! Nevertheless, it is a very interesting subject.

"Demons' Waltz" uses dropped D tuning. It features a haunting, arpeggiated intro in 4/4, played with a relatively clean sound. Then it breaks into a heavy, Metallica, "For Whom the Bell Tolls"-style 12/8 groove. The verse uses a Pantera, "Walk"-type, swing groove. Notice the diad shapes—major thirds and a minor sixth in the clean parts, the diminished 5th and major thirds later in the 12/8-swing chorus.

The entire song form is A-BBCB-DEF-DEF-BB-AA. Yeah, this looks like a mess at first, but it's really not that bad. The form is dominated by an ABA idea, or intro/main song section/outro. In other words, it's like a mini-song sandwiched inside the clean, 4/4 intro and outro parts. Just like peeling away the layers of an onion, ignore the "A's" for a moment and that alphabetical nightmare there begins to look a little more manageable. The whole middle section, in 12/8, includes intro and outro sections of its own. Consider the "BBCB" part that comes next as the "12/8 intro." This is followed by verse/pre-chorus/chorus, repeat. So that's "DEF-DEF." Then the 12/8 intro figure becomes the 12/8 outro, "BB" (it's an abbreviated version). And to wrap it up, we come back full circle, to the clean, arpeggiated 4/4 intro as an outro. That's one twisted onion!

DEMONS' WALTZ 44 45
(Song #11)

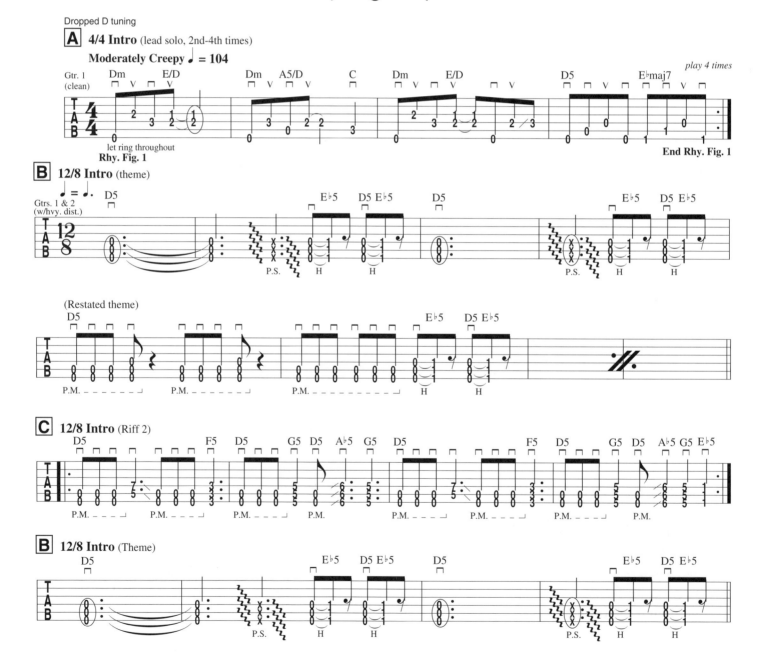

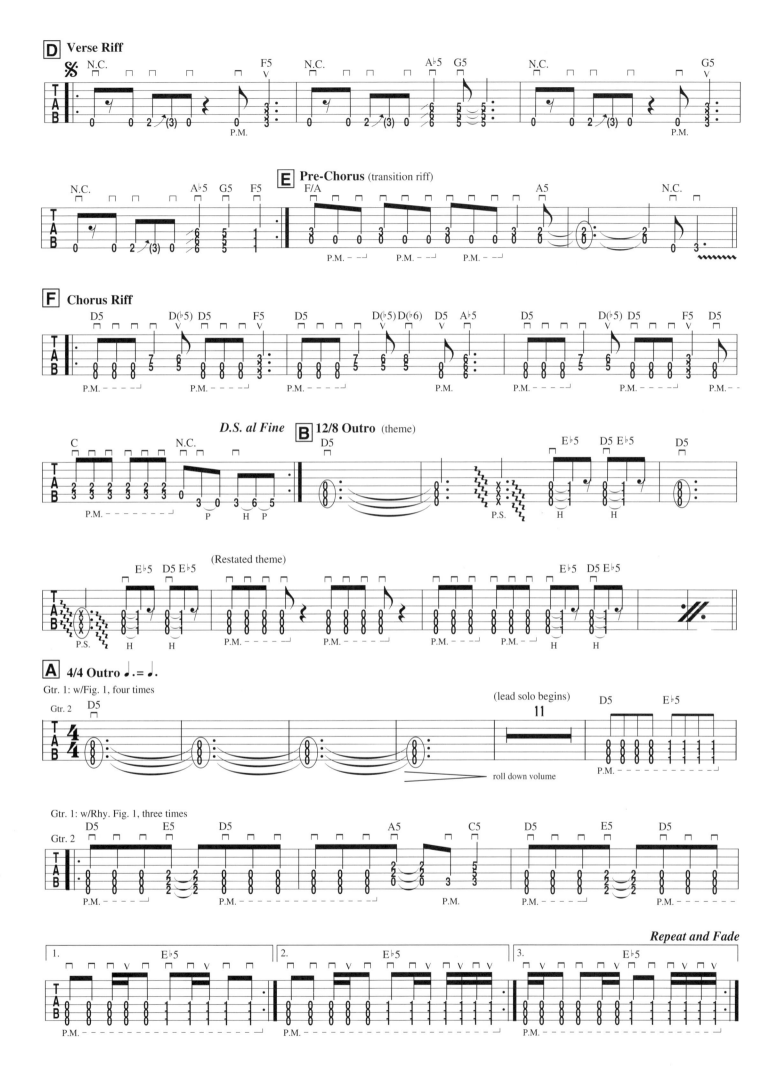

CHAPTER 12

NOTES ON "BABYLON"

Babylon is a full-length instrumental tune in F#m that applies the concepts and techniques shown throughout the *Metal Rhythm Guitar* method, including power chord and single note riffs, progressions, 12/8 and 4/4 time as well as 2/4 and 3/4 "missing beat" measures, half time, various diads, full major and minor barre chords, 7th chords, arpeggiation, downstroke as well as alternating and accent picking, all sorts of sixteenth note "offbeat" syncopations, rhythmic patterns, etc.

The structure of "Babylon" is a little more complex, with a separate intro section, a verse/chorus/ verse/ chorus song-type section, an acoustic interlude, an accent section that acts as a bridge, a special "new verse" section that is completely unrelated to the previous verses, another set of transitional breaks and the final guitar solo, or finalé. In a nutshell, it kicks off fast, breaks down into half time, then builds it back up to the final climactic battle—a musical Armageddon. Learn each part separately, then play along with the recording. Also, you may notice that Babylon is somewhat distinct in that there are an unusual number of tempo changes. But it all works together, and that's what counts.

Read a section below and then listen to the corresponding portion of the tune, in order to latch on to the main points at work in Babylon. Then go on to the next one.

A | **Intro**: The intro section is a fast-paced 12/8 groove. The key is F#m. Basically, the lead guitar phrase climbs up with each phrase, only to be slammed back down to the tonic with a simple set of ♭VII5-IV5-i5 accents. After four repetitions, the rhythm guitar, bass and drums, join the fray in a simplified version of that opening lead guitar line. The intro section ends with a longer series of accents, then holds on ♭V for a count off into a new half-time, 4/4 groove.

B | **Verse**: Although the pace is actually a bit more slower than exact half time, the variation isn't discernible. First, the bass and drums set up the groove, then the rhythm guitar enters with its basic rhythmic motif—four sixteenths and a staccato quarter note. After this short introduction, the verse begins with the lead guitar melody. Harmonically, you can see that the rhythm section implies a F#-F#-E-F# pattern, or i-i-♭VII-i for each four-bar phrase, even though no chords are played. Listen for this overall tonal movement, or progression. The verse "intro" is six bars. The verse itself is eight bars long, made up of a repeated four-bar phrase. Also notice the rhythmic patterns at work in the fills at the end of measures two, four, six, and eight.

C | **Chorus**: The verse opens directly to the chorus. Here, notice the same basic ♭VII-IV-i idea recalled from the intro. Now it is in a new environment with completely different rhythms. It also blends in the passing ♭II chord, introduced in the verse. The first chorus is four bars long, in an ABAC riff structure. (In other words, there are two, two-bar phrases which use different ending tags.)

At this point, it repeats back for the second verse and chorus. The second chorus, however, is doubled. This time, the form is ABAD-ABAE, (allowing that C still stands for the chorus ending which led back to the verse). More importantly, the ending of the last phrase is actually the beginning of the next section, so the two are woven together. (Unlike standard phrasing, where the full eight bars would be completed, then a next section begins.)

D **Acoustic Interlude**: An *interlude* is a short section that comes between two other, similar sections. Here it acts as a temporary breathing space. The acoustic guitars blend an arpeggiated F♯m with a descending bass line in the blues scale. In the second half, the tempo begins to slowly increase and tension builds. *Accel.* stands for "accelerando," the musical term for speeding up (same root as the word accelerate). *Poco á Poco* means "little by little."

E **Bridge Accents**: Brutal, unison accents destroy the calm that preceded. This accenting section is based on a one-bar riff. The form is ABAC-ABD, where D is a full-fledged lead fill in the F♯m blues scale. Then, the whole thing repeats. The single 3/4 measure near the end is woven into the fabric of the music, such that you probably won't even notice it unless you count it out.

F **New Verse**: Here the tempo relaxes a bit, as we settle into a brand new groove. Notice the octave-diad tag, marking off the end of each four bar phrase. The third time around, however, a rather rude interruption chops off the measure mid-way, and a crescendo builds up to the next part.

G **Solo Breaks**: The lead guitar starts its ascent here. Rhythmically, there is no drumbeat, only accents and a background count keeping the pulse—hence the term "breaks." The progression is i-♭VI-IV-V which is played twice.

H **Finale**: This is the climax. The progression is a long eight-bar monstrosity that uses classical chord resolution to help propel it to its final resting place. (For more on chord resolution, see *Metal Lead Guitar Volume 2.*) To get the ending rhythm up to speed, you may want to practice each few measures separately as a speed exercise, then begin putting them together. And one more thing. If you get cramping or pain in the tendons of your hands, stop! A little burning is OK, but don't hurt yourself. Try playing a little more relaxed, with less pressure on the fretboard and perhaps hold the pick a little more loosely. At the end, the term *Ritard* is used. This means to slow down. And the *fermata* symbol, or "bird's eye," above the last two chords indicates that the chord should be held for an indefinite period of time. That's it! Now it's time to get out your guitar!

BABYLON ◆46
(Song #12)

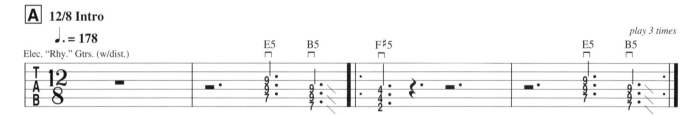

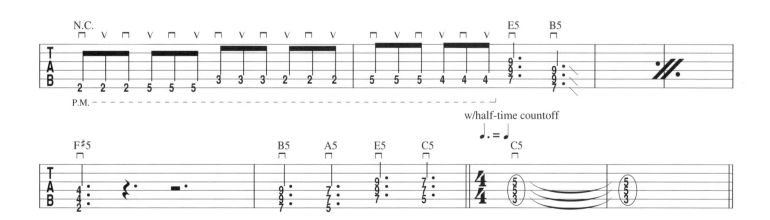

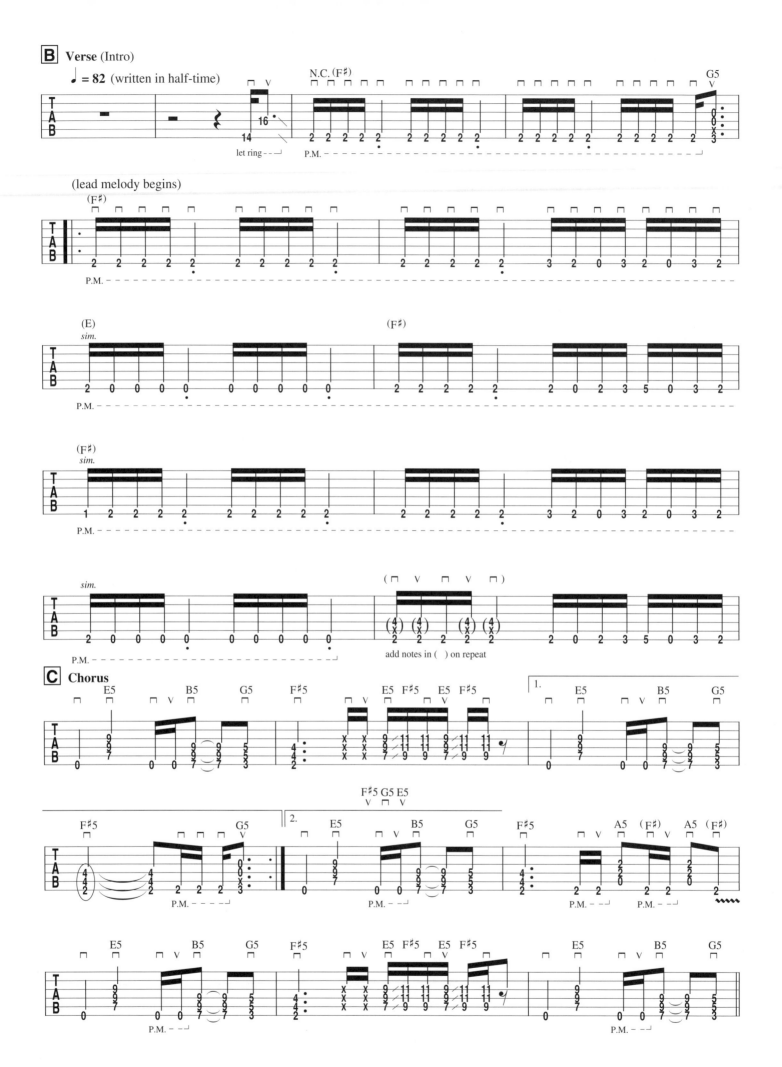

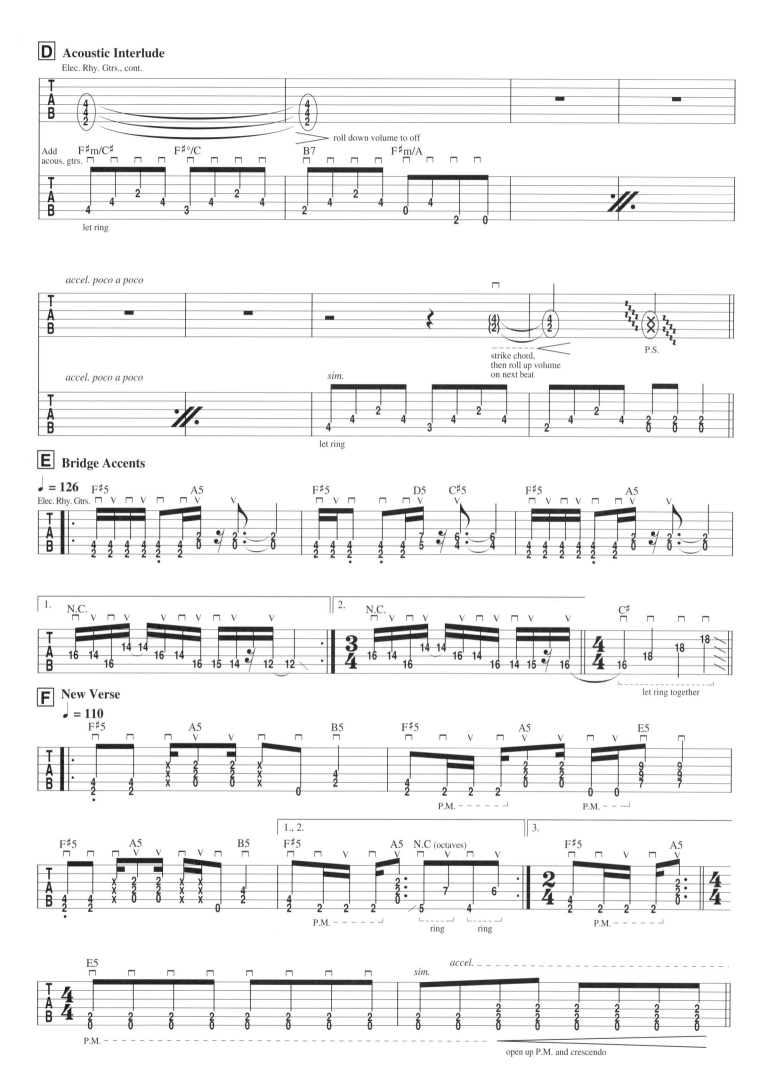

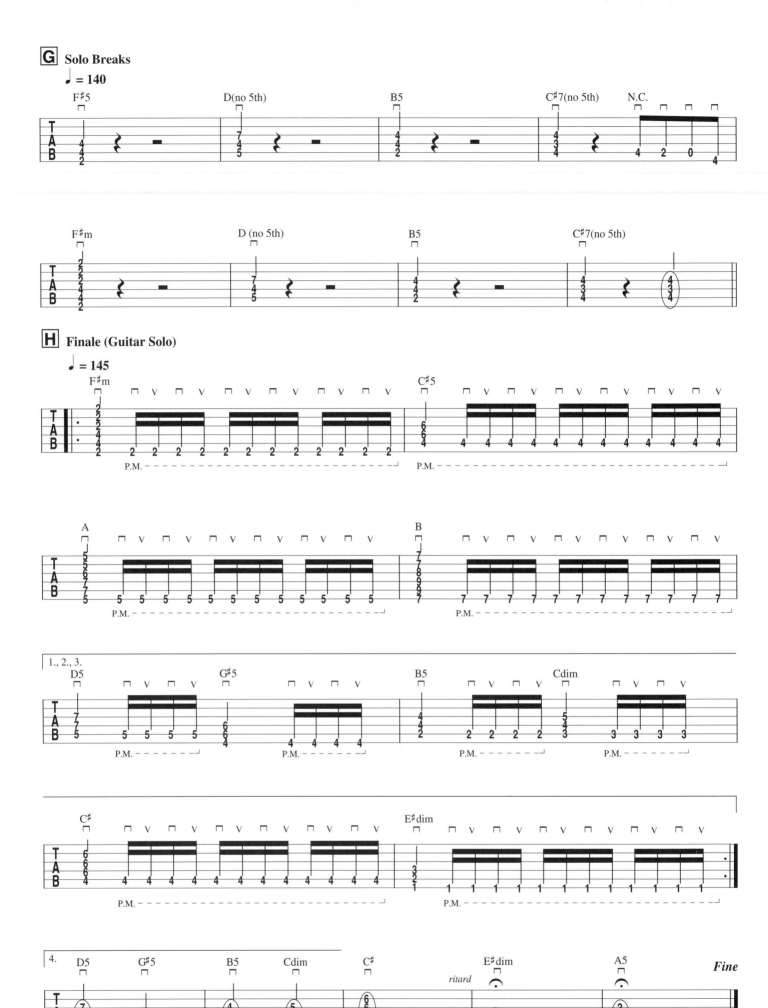

G Solo Breaks

H Finale (Guitar Solo)

Congratulations! You made it through Volume Two!

For more practice with faster, endurance-building rhythms and riffs, see *Thrash Guitar Method*.

To learn all about lead guitar soloing, see *Metal Lead Guitar, Volume One*.

For basic lead technique presented in a video format, see *Beginning Rock Lead Guitar*.

For a collection of metal tricks and techniques, see *Metal Guitar Tricks*.

For an in-depth lead technique analysis and speed builder, see *Speed Mechanics for Lead Guitar*.

KEEPING TABS ON YOUR OWN KILLER RIFFS

You know the drill. Write 'em down! There's no such thing as a bad riff. Old, tired riffs are bridges to new, inspired riffs. Play them backwards, upside down, and sideways. You can find a good idea in just about anything. This page will help you get started, but don't stop here. Get a book of manuscript paper and fill it up. Also, try recording them on a tape recorder.

NOTE NAMES ON THE FRETBOARD

The grids below show the positions of the natural notes all over the fretboard, in standard tuning. Flats and sharps are used to name all fret positions between the natural names. A flat sign (♭) lowers the pitch one fret. A sharp sign (♯) raises the pitch one fret. So all notes not labelled below can actually have two names—the flat of the note one fret higher, or the sharp of the note one fret lower.

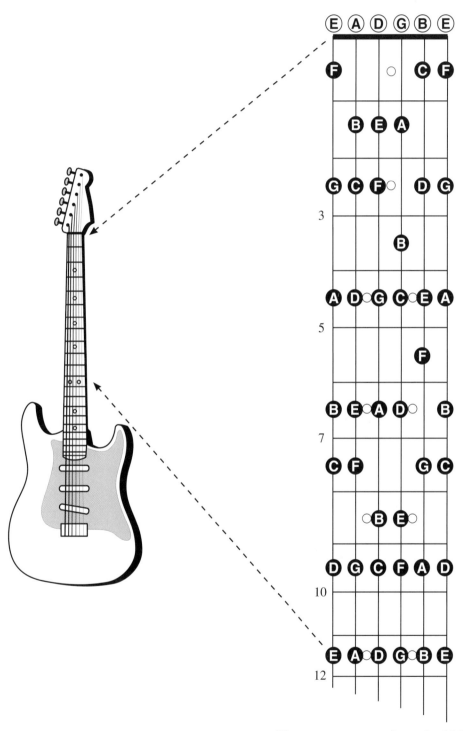

The pattern repeats above the 12th fret.
All notes are one octave higher.
(For example: 6th string, 13th fret is F, 15th fret is G, etc.)

NOTATION GUIDE

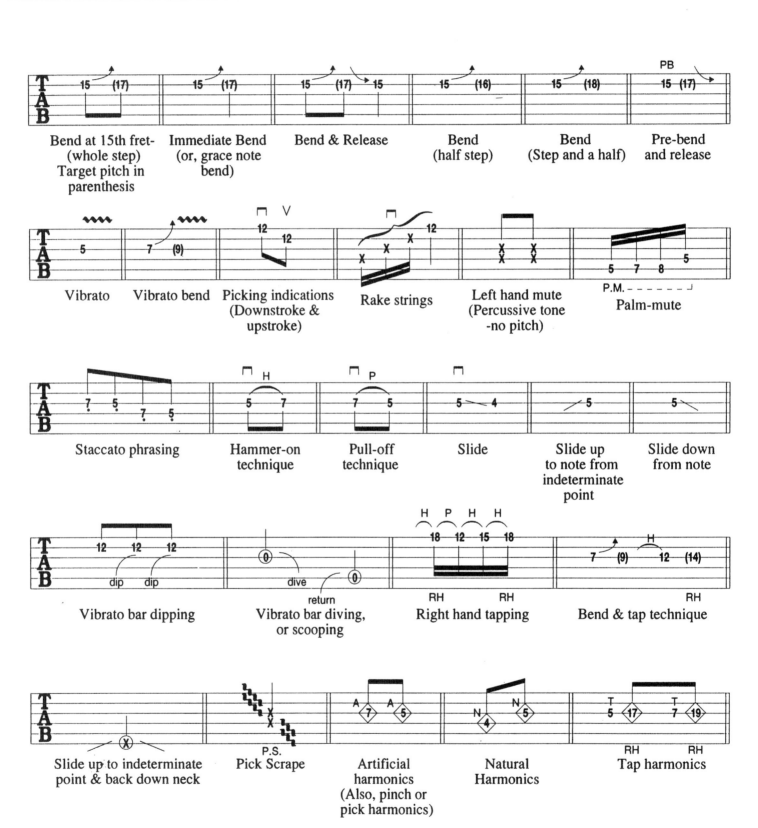

GLOSSARY OF TERMS

Scale. A particular set of notes beginning on one pitch, called the root, and continuing up to the octave of that root note. A seven tone scale is called a *diatonic* scale, and a five tone scale is a *pentatonic* scale. Also, *relative* scales are scales that share the same notes, but use different roots. *Parallel* scales share the same root, but use different notes.

Mode. A type of scale created by displacing the root of another scale. Modes can be created from any scale.

Tone. Generally, tone refers to the "treblyness" or "bassyness" of a sound. As used in this method, *tone* refers to the numbered relationship of a pitch to the root note of the scale. For example 1, 2, ♭3, or root, second and minor third are *tones*.

Note. A specific pitch, identified by a letter name. For example, A, C, F♯.

Rhythm. Generally, the whole timing aspect and length of notes. Specifically, can also refer to a *certain* sequence of timing values. For example, a *rhythm* of eighth notes.

Beat. The underlying pulse in music, in relation to which, the length and timing of notes is measured.

Riff. A short, self-contained musical thought, or phrase which appears repeatedly and plays an important role in a song. Common to rock and metal.

Lick. Refers to rock and metal lead guitar phrases that generally involve string bending or other guitar techniques. A loosely defined term, licks are also sometimes called riffs.

Chord. More than one note sounding together at the same time.

Arpeggio. The notes of a chord played one after another, in sequence.

Harmony. Generally refers to a *secondary melody* which supports and strengthens the main melody. In its widest sense, harmony is two or more notes sounding together.

Interval. The distance between two notes. The steps of the major scale are used to name intervals, as in a *major third* or *perfect fifth*. Also, a *whole step* is an interval of two frets, a half step is an interval of one fret.

Chromatic. Using every half step, as opposed to diatonic, which would follow the steps of the major or minor scale.

Form. Refers to the overall, or large scale structure of music. Letters, starting with A, B, C, etc. are used as variables to denote different sections of music. For example, form AABA is the basic song form, with A standing for a verse and chorus section and B standing for a bridge and/or solo section.

MORE GREAT TITLES FROM TROY STETINA

FRETBOARD MASTERY

Familiarizes you with all the shapes you need to know by applying them in real musical examples, thereby reinforcing and reaffirming your newfound knowledge.
00695331 Book/CD Pack $19.99

HARD ROCK
A STEP-BY-STEP BREAKDOWN OF GUITAR STYLES AND TECHNIQUES

Learn the riffs and solos of the greatest guitarists in hard rock! 8 songs are taught: Living After Midnight • Round and Round • Smoke on the Water • You Really Got Me • and more. Includes jam-along songs and practice tips. 1 hour, 36 minutes.
00320428 DVD $19.95

METAL LEAD GUITAR PRIMER

Learn metal guitar the best way - by playing music! This primer for the beginning lead guitarist builds the solid musical and technical foundation you'll need as it prepares you for Metal Lead Guitar Vol. 1 with several metal 'jams'. Whether trading licks with the pre-recorded leads, or soloing by yourself, these rhythm tracks with full band accompaniment will make you sound great and they're fun to play! A great starter book – no experience necessary! Includes tablature. 48-minute audio accompaniment.
00660316 Book/CD Pack $19.95

METAL LEAD GUITAR

This intense metal method teaches you the elements of lead guitar technique with an easy to understand, player-oriented approach. The metal concepts, theory, and musical principles are all applied to real metal licks, runs and full compositions. Learn at your own pace through 12 fully transcribed heavy metal solos from simple to truly terrifying! Music and examples demonstrated on CD. "One of the most thorough" and "one of the best rock series currently available" – *Guitar Player* magazine.
00699321 Volume 1 – Book/CD Pack $19.99
00699322 Volume 2 – Book/CD Pack $19.95

METAL RHYTHM GUITAR

Because rhythm and timing lie at the foundation of everything you play, its importance can't be underestimated. This series will give you that solid foundation you need. Starts with simple upbeat rhythms for the beginner and moves step by step into advanced syncopations – all demonstrated with seriously heavy metal examples that have practical applications to today's styles. Tablature. Music and examples demonstrated on CD.
00699319 Volume 1 – Book/CD Pack $19.99
00699320 Volume 2 – Book/CD Pack $19.95

SPEED MECHANICS FOR LEAD GUITAR

Learn the fastest ways to achieve speed and control, secrets to make your practice time really count, and how to open your ears and make your musical ideas more solid and tangible. Packed with over 200 vicious exercises. 89-minute audio.
00699323 Book/CD Pack $19.95

TROY STETINA – THE SOUND AND THE STORY
ALL-ACCESS GUITAR INSTRUCTION   *Fret12*

Topics covered include: the path to unlimited speed, control and articulation • ultimate shred picking secrets • non-standard phrasing ideas and bending approaches • secrets to playing in the pocket and building engaging riffs • arrangement tips and compositional ideas • and more. Approximately 3 hrs., 30 min.
00321271 DVD $39.95

THRASH GUITAR METHOD

by Troy Stetina and Tony Burton

Let the mosh begin! This truly radical method book takes you from slow grinding metal up to the fastest thrashing. Syncopation, shifting accents, thrash theory, progressions, chromatic 'ear-twisting' melodic dissonances, shifting time signatures, harmony, and more. CD features bull band accompaniment for all musical examples so that you can play along with the band. Fully transcribed in tablature!
00697218 Book/CD Pack $19.95

TOTAL ROCK GUITAR
A COMPLETE GUIDE TO LEARNING ROCK GUITAR

Total Rock Guitar is a unique and comprehensive source for learning rock guitar, designed to develop both lead and rhythm playing. This book/CD pack covers: getting a tone that rocks; open chords, power chords and barre chords; riffs, scales and licks; string bending, strumming, palm muting, harmonics and alternate picking; all rock styles; and much more. The examples in the book are in standard notation with chord grids and tablature, and the CD includes full-band backing for all 22 songs.
00695246 Book/CD Pack $19.99

200 ROCK LICKS

GUITAR LICKS GOLDMINE

featuring Greg Harrison, Matthew Schroeder and Troy Stetina

A *Guitar Licks Goldmine* awaits in this incredible rock collection! This DVD is jam-packed with killer lead lines, phrases, and riffs personally taught to you by professional guitarists Greg Harrison, Matthew Schroeder, and Troy Stetina. From classic rock to modern metal, each and every authentic lick includes: a walk-through explanation by a pro guitarist; note-for-note on-screen tablature; normal and slow-speed performance demos. 4 hours, 14 minutes.
00320930 DVD $24.99

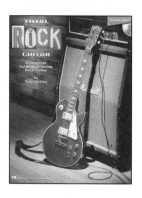

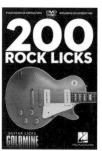

HAL•LEONARD®
CORPORATION

7777 W. BLUEMOUND RD. P.O. BOX 13819 MILWAUKEE, WI 53213

www.halleonard.com

Prices, contents, and availability subject to change without notice.